- **Are You Feeling Guilty About a Flirtation That's Gotten Out of Hand?**

- **Are You Having Trouble Deciding Whether to Take That Promising Job Offer?**

- **Should You Take Chances With Your Life or Seek the Secure Way?**

Every night you dream the answers to these and other questions that fill your waking hours. But often the solutions your sleeping mind offers you are hidden in symbolism. How can you break the dream code? Let the zodiac be your key to the wisdom buried in your unconscious mind! All it takes is the knowledge in SUN SIGNS AND DREAMS. Then stretch out, close your eyes, and dream your way to a wonderful future!

Sun Signs and Dreams

by

Doris Kaye

A SIGNET BOOK

NEW AMERICAN LIBRARY

A DIVISION OF PENGUIN BOOKS USA INC.

NAL BOOKS ARE AVAILABLE AT QUANTITY DISCOUNTS
WHEN USED TO PROMOTE PRODUCTS OR SERVICES.
FOR INFORMATION PLEASE WRITE TO PREMIUM MARKETING DIVISION,
NEW AMERICAN LIBRARY, 1633 BROADWAY,
NEW YORK, NEW YORK 10019.

SIGNET TRADEMARK REG. U.S. PAT. OFF. AND FOREIGN COUNTRIES
REGISTERED TRADEMARK—MARCA REGISTRADA
HECHO EN DRESDEN, TN, U.S.A.

SIGNET, SIGNET CLASSIC, MENTOR, ONYX, PLUME, MERIDIAN
and NAL BOOKS are published by New American Library, a division of
Penguin Books USA Inc., 1633 Broadway, New York, New York 10019

First Signet Printing, September, 1977

4 5 6 7 8 9

PRINTED IN THE UNITED STATES OF AMERICA

For Virginia Mary Scanlan

Contents

Chapter 1

The Link Between Dreams and Astrology

The blend of dream interpretation and astrology is doubly revealing and rewarding. If you understand yourself through astrology, you can better understand your dreams—why you dream what you dream, and how to use this knowledge to improve your life.

A dream is the most personal of all the experiences you have. No one else can actually participate in your dreams; you may dream *of* others, but not *with* others. A dream is also your own unique creation. You are the playwright, the star performer, and also the audience in the nightly drama of your dreams. And, whether or not you remember them, you have dreams every single night of your life. As a matter of fact it has been well established through scientific experiments in sleep monitoring on controlled groups of individuals that when dreams are prevented these people show an ever-increasing anxiety, irritation, lack of coordination, and general deterioration. So, from the standpoint of health and sanity, dreams are a must!

There are as many kinds of dreams as there are people, though these can be classified under various specific categories of dreams: action dreams (when you are running, leaping, flying, physically moving about), passive dreams (when you observe dream events that happen *to* you). There are insecurity dreams, frustration dreams, recurring dreams, escape dreams, precognitive dreams, and many other types.

Though not all psychologists agree on dream symbolism, or on the interpretation of these nightly perambulations, it has been established that of the three states of being—the unconscious, the subconscious, and the conscious—the first two of these are the source of your dreams.

The unconscious, considered by Jung to represent the racial memory of man ("the unconscious is the unwritten history of mankind from time unrecorded"), is the source of your deepest instincts—instincts of which you may be unaware, that are expressed automatically, and are buried deep in your psyche.

The subconscious, though not so deeply embedded in your psyche as the unconscious, can still operate with little or no conscious perception on your part and usually represents your desires. The subconscious can, of course, also operate during waking hours. Well-known examples of subconscious desires being expressed in the awake state are the hypochondriac who uses imaginary ailments as a bid for attention—the subconscious desire being to gain the spotlight—or the practical joker who plays embarrassing or painful tricks on another, stemming from the subconscious desire to hurt.

The conscious state needs little explanation, as this is readily recognizable by you and operates through your will, thinking processes, decision-making ability, and all other facets of everyday living of which you are fully aware.

Astrology is often referred to as the oldest psychological technique known to man and, is, by its very nature, deeply involved in the unconscious, subconscious, and conscious states of individuals. If you have read astrological literature, you have noted phrases such as "you are naturally inclined to be cautious" or "you are inherently ambitious" or "you are innately competitive"—all of which refer to the unconscious state and comprise traits or qualities that are as natural to you as breathing and which can be modified, controlled, or changed only by an act of the will: a conscious act.

A person's subconscious is revealed through astrology in terms of desires, whether the desire is for tangibles (recognition, power, material success) or intangibles (love, security, peace). Subconscious desires may be expressed negatively—such as the desire for justice expressed through vengeance—or positively, such as the desire for love expressed through loving others.

The conscious state of an individual is astrologically delineated via the strength or weakness of his will, his mentality and ability to handle daily demands and decisions.

In your dreams, it is your subconscious that invariably writes the script; and as your subconscious reflects your desires, there's a lot of camouflage involved in your dreams—for one of your deepest desires is to protect yourself. Although this specific urge for self-protection has roots in the unconscious (the instinct for survival), it bridges into the subconscious, as well. This is why in dream interpretation the various people who wander in and out of your dreams can sometimes be projections of *you*—particularly if they are behaving badly, or you are punishing them for something; it's often the guilt feeling at work, with your subconscious protecting you from the admission of your own transgressions or lacks—directing the guilt away from you and onto another.

Jung has stated that "it is not easy to lay down any special rules for the type of dream compensation. Its character is always bound up with the whole nature of the individual." Astrology deals with *the whole nature of the individual.* The twelve signs of the Zodiac produce many and varied types, and interpreting the dreams of a Piscean, for example, would need different standards than those used in interpreting the dreams of a Sagittarian.

It should be pointed out here that the individual birth chart, calculated for the date, time, and place of birth, is the most detailed and meaningful in terms of dealing with "the whole nature of the individual." However, Sun sign characteristics and traits are very basic, as are the desire-instincts and subconscious motives of each of the twelve Sun signs. By understanding your deepest instincts and your subconscious desires through both astrology and dreams, you are in a better position to utilize your special abilities and talents, consciously, for a better life.

Yes, you are the author of your dream plots, but how are you as a translator?

Chapter 2

What Are Your Dreams Telling You?

In general, your dreams tend to reflect unresolved problems, subconscious fears, insecurities, very often things you do not face up to in your everyday conscious living. "Good night and sweet dreams" is a pleasant way to send a person off to bed, but actually there is not that high a percentage of enjoyable dreams. Your nightly dreams are often likely to produce a batch of apparently unimportant or even ridiculous details and unrelated incidents, or to be so vague, confusing, or disjointed that upon awakening you find it difficult to recall any general theme to the night's dream events. There is, however, a meaning to even the most unintelligible dream.

Dreams also reflect the ego and personality of the dreamer (which is not surprising, inasmuch as *you* are the focal point of your dreams). If you have a direct, uncomplicated nature, your dreams are likely to be direct and uncomplicated—though even the most seemingly uncomplicated person can have quirky little areas in his psyche, which do show up in dreams. However, the more inverted, obtuse, devious, or involved the individual may be, the more his dreams will reflect these qualities.

Dreams can often refer, in their own oblique way, to a particular problem—invariably a current, immediate problem—about which the individual has made an incorrect or inaccurate conscious judgment; in such instances the subconscious attempts to set the dreamer straight on the matter. This frequently occurs when the dreamer experiences a similar problem but in a very different set of dream circumstances, through which additional light is shed on the matter. Subsequent dreams on the same general theme often occur until the dreamer gets the point of what his subconscious is trying to transmit—another example of the subconscious always in there, attempting to help or protect you. It should be emphasized, though, that the subconscious is entirely amoral in its effort on your behalf, and should not be confused with conscience, moral principles, or ethics.

The most important part of dream interpretation is determining the strongest impression the dream makes on *you*. How you feel as the result of a specific dream is the clue—which is why it can be inaccurate to state arbitrarily that a specific dream event or dream object has a specific meaning for all who dream about it. For example, a dream of flying through the air (all on your own—no plane) could be exhilarating to someone of an adventurous, freedom-loving nature—but a fearful dream experience to an individual who is ultra security-minded and who loathes the thought of ever leaving the ground even in the most super 747.

Even if you dream of beautiful scenery, lovely people, peaceful surroundings, the dream can be accompanied by a nagging worry or foreboding amidst all the loveliness; the emotional impression the dream makes on you is what counts. (In such a dream, for instance, the dreamer may have a subconscious guilt feeling about a pleasant development—of recent date or shortly to come—or may feel undeserving of good things—which could very well stem from childhood conditioning—and so on.)

Despite the specific content of your dreams, look for the focal impression the dream makes on you.

As your psyche consists primarily of images, dreams also express through images. Here again, what the image means to *you* is what's important. If you love dogs, a dog in your dream can be a love image; if you dislike or fear dogs, dreaming of one can make it an image of a person or condition or something in yourself you dislike or fear.

The dream categories discussed in Chapter 3 are based on predominant themes or impressions that such dreams reveal to *you.* For example, an escape dream may consist of running, a last-minute leap onto a train or plane, finding yourself in an entirely new environment among a group of total strangers, discovering an open door or a key to a door after a seeming dream eternity of seeking it. In short, any dream that makes a strong impression on you of your having escaped (or attempting to escape) from a problem, situation, person, or whatever, is an escape dream.

As you analyze your dreams, look for the dominant theme among the various categories. This will reveal a situation in your life of importance at the moment—and only you can determine what that is. Then look to see if the dream has provided additional insight into the situation, or a solution to the problem—although it must be pointed out that dreams rarely provide cut-and-dried solutions, but do give valuable clues to the reality of a problem. Once you have realistically appraised the matter, it becomes the job of your conscious will to take over the work and produce the solution.

If you are one of the many who do not remember their dreams, who retain only nebulous bits and pieces of the night's dream events, you can improve your waking memory by making a firm resolve just as you go to sleep—"I will remember my dreams"—much in the same way that you can "set" your mind to wake up at a specific hour.

Chapter 3

Dream Categories

Confinement Dreams In this type of dream you find yourself in some place from which you cannot escape—and you usually have no idea of how you got there. It may be a prison, hospital, cave, room, building, frequently just an unidentifiable *place* from which there is no exit and your reaction is one of panic. In the first place, don't interpret this kind of dream as an indication that you are going to be arrested or hospitalized. Your "imprisonment" is symbolic and self-imposed, and your subconscious is reminding you of this. You have a hidden fear of some sort related to a matter that you do not wish to have known (infidelity? infraction of a rule, regulation, or law? something sneaky you did to another behind his/her back?). In any case, here you are trapped by your own conscience operating *through* your subconscious. If you have not got out of this confinement area before you wake up, or if your waking impression retains the panic feeling, then it behooves you to do whatever you can to straighten out the matter from which this dream stemmed, or to bring it out in the open if that is possible or feasible; otherwise it will remain in your psyche and you can expect more of the same in future dreams. Geminis, Ariens, and Aquarians are subject to this type of dream.

* * *

Insecurity Dreams By far the most frequent among all dreams! Who of us is not insecure about something? Money, job, relationships, life-in-a-big-city, and so on, all provide much food for the insecurity dream. Such a dream may find you falling, losing your purse or wallet, having your car or valuables stolen, slipping off a curbstone or down the stairs, being struck by lightning or in an earthquake, being lost in a strange place—any situation in which you feel insecure, baffled, startled, uneasy, worried. Also, should you find yourself in a dream suddenly strolling stark naked through Times Square, you may wish to give this dream a sexual connotation, but actually it's an insecurity dream. What you are insecure about in your dream usually has no direct connection to the actual source of the insecurity in your conscious life. Parallel dreams (those which coincide exactly with the real details of a specific problem) are very rare. So, this sort of dream would concern one of your major insecurities and, as in all dreams, the focal point is your own reaction to the dream event.

Reasonable calm while you are immersed in the disaster or experiencing the loss (or nonchalance over your public nudity!) is your subconscious telling you that you can indeed cope with strange and sudden events, should they occur. If, on the other hand, you feel shattered by the dream scene, your subconscious is dramatically impressing on you your *need* to consciously learn to cope—perhaps by being more cautious, practical, provident or using more common sense in assessing a major cause of insecurity in your life. Incidentally, our dreams can sometimes reflect conscious impressions we've experienced in the recent past; our subconscious takes this material and relates it to one of our own particular problems. For instance, the evening news may impress you with the details of a terrible plane crash or train wreck and you subsequently dream you are in a similar accident. This does not necessarily indicate a warning against train or plane travel, but merely that you may be insecure about a business deal, or a relationship, and you subconsciously fear that should the matter not work out as hoped, you would be in effect wrecked. No particular sign has the edge on the insecurity dream; we all have them.

Frustration Dreams These first three dream categories—the confinement dream, the insecurity dream, and the frustration dream—have their basic root in anxiety. As global, national, local, and personal affairs become more and more complicated, anxiety dreams become more and more prevalent. The key to recognizing a frustration dream is that in such a dream you are prevented from completing something you start. Added to this is often a receding memory of the dream, even as you awake, so you feel frustrated even more by not being able to recall what it was that frustrated you in the dream: a fine way to begin the day! Frequently, a communication of some sort is involved in a frustration dream; you never quite get to the point of telling an individual in your dream something of importance—or the other person is to tell you something, but the dream ends before he or she does so. There is also the sort of frustration dream where you never arrive at a place you're anxiously trying to get to, or you're meeting someone who doesn't show up, or you get lost on the way to the meeting place.

The incompleted act is the keynote of the frustration dream, whether in the realms of the mind, emotions, or sex. You can find the correlation between this type of dream and a frustrating condition or person in your everyday life by recognizing the correlation between your reactions in the dream and your reactions in your waking hours to the source of your frustration. It may be that the actual situation in your life is, for the moment, unchangeable—the assumption being that if you could change it you would. Perhaps you have a family responsibility or a repressive boss. Your subconscious can provide clues, in the dream, to alternative action that might improve the situation in your life. For example, a dream in which you never reach a destination that you're trying to get to throughout the dream, because somewhere along the way you're faced with a choice of routes—or a dream in which you unexpectedly find yourself in a strange environment—can reflect your subconscious pointing the way to an alternative, an outlet for the frustration.

As with all dreams, these anxiety type dreams are significant for the impression they make on *you*—for your reactions to frustrating dream events in terms of whether they stimulate you toward creative thinking in finding solutions, or have a deflating, restrictive effect. Virgos and Capricorns tend to have frustration dreams.

Passive Dreams These might be described as dreams-within-a-dream experiences, in which you are the observer of what occurs to you and/or others. In such dreams, which may unfold almost any type of event, you are truly the passive watcher and do not experience emotions, reactions, sensations; you are on the sidelines, so to speak, an observer viewing the action. In this sort of dream, your subconscious is being very objective and is reminding you to use more objectivity and detachment in your outlook on matters about which, in your conscious state, you might be overly emotional.

Whatever the content of your passive dream, try to recall the actions and dialogue of the people in your dream, including yourself, and relate this to a special situation or problem. This can give you a more realistic understanding of the matter, which—

during your waking hours—is probably being obscured by your tendency to wear emotional blinders. In the passive dream, you watch as various events involve you and others, but do not experience the pain or the joy, whichever is appropriate to the situation; you are merely a remote, impartial monitor of the action. This in itself is a clue from your subconscious to detach yourself from subjective emotionalism in a specific matter, to depersonalize. Cancerians and Scorpios are prone to this sort of dream.

Action Dreams These dreams often have a tinge of other dream categories as well. Are you running *to* something or *away* from something? Are you stimulated by the dream activity, or do you wake up exhausted after a dream experience of chasing about after someone or something? If there is anxiety overlaying the action, this may be an insecurity or frustration dream, even though its physical activity puts it in the action class, too. In this sort of dream, you do not watch, observe, or passively accept events; you act. Climbing endless stairs is an action dream, so is running for a moving vehicle. If you catch up with the moving vehicle, get on board, and feel relieved, there's a tinge of the escape dream here; and this invariably represents a problem or situation from which you would like to escape and probably can, inasmuch as catching up with that "escape" vehicle is your subconscious telling you there's a way out. On the other hand, if you never board the train or whatever, or the top of the stairs is not reached in your dream sequence, there's a tinge of the frustration dream in this one. Action dreams also can comprise your participation in a sport, or you are dancing, jumping, jogging, somehow moving about physically in a way that *feels* in your dream just as it does in your waking hours—as opposed to that veiled sense of not-quite-full participation in events, featured in other types of dreams.

In the action dream, your subconscious is telling you (aside from the obvious message that you should get out of your ivory tower and into the mainstream) that you should be the one who determines your own life style; you may need to become more aggressive in initiating action and, hence, less passive in allowing events initiated by others to happen *to* you. This sort of dream is supposed to be a stimulus to decisive action in your waking hours—at least your subconscious is trying to tell you to get going and *do* something! Taureans and Librans can learn from action dreams; Ariens and Sagittarians are most responsive to the action dream.

Recurring Dreams As the word implies, recurring dreams are those in which a familiar theme is reenacted more than once. As the dreamer, you recognize the theme or the scene of the dream plot as it recurs, with a feeling of "here we go again." Obviously, your subconscious is trying to tell you something that you are either refusing to face or are not perceptive enough to latch on to! Recurring dreams are extremely meaningful and if your subconscious takes the trouble to dredge up the same old patterns again and again, the least you can do is give this sort of dream careful analysis. Many a clue shows up in a recurring dream if you will but see them.

The interesting thing is that most recurring dreams do not have a conclusion or an ending, naturally—for they represent a condition in your life, or a problem, for which you have not as yet written the final scene, awake or asleep. The subject matter of such dreams varies and you must relate it to the condition or problem in question. If there is another individual in this dream, note whether he or she is acting out of character (your jolliest friend being dreary in your dream, or your easygoing boss behaving like a tyrant). If that person is acting out of character, then he or she is merely an extension of yourself, with your subconscious sparing you the blow of self-criticism. Nevertheless, this would relate to a trait or quality in yourself that needs an overhaul and your subconscious is patiently reminding you of this, periodically. If the person in your dream *is* behaving in character—just as he or she behaves in everyday life—then the meaning of the dream concerns a relationship, though not necessarily with that particular individual. That's complicated, isn't it?—and maybe that's why you haven't yet gotten the point of this dream and keep reexperiencing it. If it's a relationship that is involved, look for the *quality* of the dream relationship, to correlate it with the appropriate waking-hours relationship. For instance, you may dream of experiencing a romantic interest in some coworker who has never in the least attracted you, but this dream points up your relationship with one who really *does* attract you. Or, if your dream features an antagonism with a good friend, forget the good friend—this dream is telling you something about someone who is *not* a good friend. Whatever the substance of the recurring dream, ponder it in depth, for it does have a message from your subconscious. No particular sign is subject to this type of dream; it occurs to anyone whenever there is a need for reiterated reminders.

Escape Dreams These are probably the most enjoyable of dreams; and probably the most rare, because in general it does seem that our subconscious prefers to teach, nag, remind, suggest, or pressure us rather than give us any pleasure. Nevertheless, the escape dream does pop up now and then and invariably is a prelude to waking up in a good mood. The main theme of the escape dream is that you've gotten away from something unpleasant or dull into something enjoyable and exhilarating. Freedom is the keyword of this dream, frequently expressed through running without effort, even flying without wings, and though there is a school of thought that gives flying a sexual connotation, it is very much of the escape pattern in its break with earthbound restrictions.

This type of dream may find you in a delightful environment, without a worry in the world; or, more symbolically, you may in your dream literally escape some nameless fate by hastening through a door, jumping through a window, or driving off in a fast car. Whatever the scene, you'll recognize your escape dream if or when you have it, for you will revel in the feeling of freedom it imparts. People who are heavily burdened with responsibility and restriction in everyday life tend to experience the escape dream once in a while—a sort of bonus from their subconscious, which also serves to release built-up tensions.

Sex Dreams It's an interesting phenomenon that people rarely dream of having sex with someone they would really like to have sex with. Suddenly there's a stranger in your bed—or wherever—and though you may be madly yearning to embrace a special someone, that's not likely to be the someone you find there in your sex dream. In a sense, this dream is one of the easiest to interpret as it signifies your sex drive and the need to express it. If you have a satisfactory sex life in your waking hours, you are not so apt to experience the sex dream. This type of dream can bridge over into a frustration dream, particularly if it is not orgasmic (females tend to have nonorgasmic sex dreams more often than males, which is partly biological, partly emotional, and/or due to the female cycle). In any case, if you have frequent sex dreams, your subconscious is reminding you that you need more sex in your life; but remember, your subconscious is amoral. There is also the possibility that a preoccupation with sex in your waking hours will flood your subconscious with this theme, resulting in an occasional sex dream—though probably not as many as you'd really like. (Preoccupation with any matter in waking hours tends to preclude dreaming about it.) With regard to the partners in your sex dreams, there is usually a connection with a real person; though you may have, in your waking hours, shut off your sexual reaction to this individual. What gets tucked away in your subconscious, shows up in your dreams. If your sex dreams feature the do-it-yourself method, and if this is frequent, your subconscious is gratifying your sex drive, but in the infantile manner. There could be a message here regarding your need to work toward greater maturity if you have frequent dreams of solitary sex. Also, this could be significant in nonsexual terms, such as your desire to evade responsibility.

Sensuous Dreams Sensuous dreams are differentiated from the sex dream by the simple fact that no sexual stimulation or reactions are involved. Very often this type of dream will concern food and one of the most frequent is the dream in which you keep eating and eating and enjoying it less and less (sometimes even waking with a slight feeling of nausea). It's a clear message from your subconscious—a warning against excessive indulgence of one of your senses, not necessarily the sense of taste. Very often it will be a sweet food that, in your dream, you keep eating until you get sick; this would be a symbol for a luxury, too much of the "good life" in one form or another. A sensuous dream can also relate to your sense of smell; a pleasing scent is your subconscious savoring some little success or triumph you've recently enjoyed—an unpleasant odor relating to a disappointment or to a suspicion you're harboring about an individual or situation.

Sensuous dreams related to hearing are comparatively rare; true, the conversation of others is often audible to you in a dream, but more general sounds—such as music, thunder, waves on a shore, birds singing—are not all that frequent (when's the last time you heard music in your dreams, not to be confused with your clock-radio awakening you?). Pleasing sounds in your dreams indicate that your subconscious is reminding you of creative talents and/or spiritual truths—and very often the two are linked. This is also true of the sense of vision, for although your sight is part of all dreams (since you are watching the panorama), real clarity of vision is somewhat unusual in a dream, and the average person dreams in black and white or varying shades of muted tones. When the vision is sharp, and especially if brilliant, well-defined colors are present in a dream, your subconscious is striving to awaken your creative powers.

The sense of touch operative in a dream—holding an object, stroking, striking, or manually utilizing it—indicates evaluation. Your subconscious is emphasizing the need to examine, weigh, assess, or otherwise investigate a certain matter—most likely of a material nature, perhaps concerning your job, finances, or property. Taureans and Pisceans tend to have sensuous dreams.

Precognitive Dreams This type of dream is one in which an event featured in the dream, or a close parallel, later actually occurs in a real-life happening. Some people have a lot of this type of dream; others never experience it. Much will depend on your own receptiveness to intuitive promptings, for although the precognitive dream is not intuition per se, it seems that people who do have a well-developed capacity for intuition tend to have precognitive dreams. An exception to this may be found in the individual who scoffs at "that sort of thing," yet whose subconscious—maybe once in a lifetime—will burst through with a real on-target precognitive dream which, when it is later mirrored in the waking life, is dismissed by the skeptical dreamer as mere coincidence. In any case, when you have a precognitive dream you do not know it falls into that category until later, when the event happens in your waking state. In this dream, your subconscious is a step ahead of you, tuned into the cosmic and not limited by the immediate or by the time factor.

The subject matter of the dream may be anything, important or trifling. However, if you do have occasional dreams that turn out to be precognitive, your subconscious is letting you know that you are more visionary than you may realize. Also, it reinforces the link between cause and effect, as your actions of today can result in the events of tomorrow. Aquarians, Sagittarians, and Taureans often have precognitive dreams.

Peopled Dreams Who are all those strangers in your dreams, and why do you sometimes dream of individuals you've not seen for years? Well, there's a correlation between these people in your dreams and those in your everyday life; so pay attention to what they say or do. If you think about it that tall, fair man you dreamt of is very like one of your co-workers or a fellow student—whose appearance may actually be short and dark, but who makes the same impression on you as the tall blond of your dream. They probably share character traits, personal magnetism, etc. This sort of association goes beyond surface appearances. Look for the nitty-gritty of the dream character's personality, motives, and actions, and you'll find this corresponds to your everyday associate's basic character.

The reason so many people say they have meaningless, unimportant dreams is that they do not delve deeply enough into the correspondences between dream figures and events and those in their daily lives. Very often you encounter people in your dreams with whom, in the dream, you experience a sense of familiarity. In your dream you know this person; upon reflection after awakening, you find that you do not know him or her. However, that individual in your dream is an image—a portrayal of someone you do really know—so search for identifying clues. Such clues may also help you to categorize the person you're seeking to identify by correlation; for example, to dream of an older man or woman could signify the father or mother image, or someone in your dream who sparks off your romantic response could represent a love object. Everyone has peopled dreams; the problem is to identify these images and relate them to those in your everyday life.

Symbols in Dreams Symbolism is an important part of astrology and dreams. The four elements—fire, earth, air, and water—into which the twelve signs of the Zodiac are divided, have a correlation with your own various components. Fire represents the spirit, earth represents the material body, air corresponds to the mentality, and water to the emotions. Accordingly, in your dreams the element of water denotes an emotional situation; you may dream of swimming, sitting by a lake, luxuriating in your tub, walking in the rain—or of being in a flood! The impression made on you by a "watery" dream is what's important in the emotional matter. If you enjoy the swimming, the lake, the tub, or the rain, there is some form of emotional satisfaction present in your waking life and reflected in the dream. If you are anxious or fearful (and undoubtedly you would be if you dreamed you were in a flood!), this simply reflects an emotional and perhaps irrational fear you have, and your subconscious is bringing it to your attention: a fear, maybe, of being "engulfed" by a certain situation, most likely involving your emotions.

Dreaming of the earth element—gardening, traversing earthy areas (meadows, mountains, dirt roads, etc.)—relates to material matters: your health, job, finances, property and so on. Again, if the dream leaves a pleasant impression with you, material interests are proceeding—or can proceed—as you plan. The reverse would apply if you are unhappy in your dream's earthiness.

Dreaming of fire has spiritual significance. Of course a fire dream that included feelings of danger would hardly be enjoyable (and, indeed, would be your subconscious accenting your need for increased spiritual awareness). An undangerous dream of the element of fire relates to a spiritual awakening in process, but as yet unperceived in your conscious state. Fire is also an indication of creativity—harnessed to constructive expression, or running wild in your subconscious. A dream involving the element of air—flying (in or out of a plane), contemplating stars, sunsets, other upper-ozone-layer focuses—signifies your potenital for mental expansion: ideas, plans, long-range strategies and so on.

Other symbols in your dreams may take the form of animals, numbers, colors, abstract designs; also such objects as a flower, tree, an article of clothing—any single object which is highlighted in the dream. Dream symbolism is important to you in an explicitly personal way. To arbitrarily state, for example, that a dog represents a friend, or a cat symbolizes an enemy, could be quite inaccurate for *you*. The cat you dream of (especially if you like felines) could symbolize the presence of a comforting, supportive individual in the background of your life; or the dog might represent a challenging situation in which you are involved. A particular color featured in your dream is likely to have links with the distant past (that certain shade of pink that was your first party dress could denote a current pleasure or a small honor; that muted green that depresses you in your dream might be the color of a blanket on a sick bed you viewed as a child). Again, only you can determine the associations of the symbols in your dreams with their correlated waking-life meaning. This means careful analysis and memory explorations, on your part, to link these materials of your subconscious with reality; only then can you discover the message being transmitted by your subconscious in its use of symbolism. Not everyone dreams of symbols; Leos and Scorpios do so more often than most people.

Chapter 4

Aries
(March 21–April 20)

Your natural instincts (your unconscious) and your deepest desires, of which you are frequently unaware (your subconscious), are the sources of your dreams. Your Sun sign is the cornerstone of your individuality. Just as the fact that you are an Aries reflects in your dreams in a special, unique manner, your dreams reveal your own special, unique unconscious and subconscious states.

ARIES is a fire sign, ruled by Mars, cardinal in quality (which means action-oriented). It is the first sign of the Zodiac, a fact which many acclaim as the source of your competitive "me-first" attitude. Certainly your temperament reflects the positive, dynamic, impulsive traits associated with the element of fire and the warrior planet, Mars. You are at your best in an active, progressive life style; you can be impatient, restless, frustrated, when the pace is too slow or you are boxed in by rigid schedules and restrictive tasks. You are quick to rise to a challenge, derive satisfaction from overcoming obstacles, and are ever eager to be on your way toward new and exciting goals. You're a great one for initiating the action; a natural trend-setter, you relish your role as "pioneer," whether this means launching a new business venture, creating an innovative art form—or designing a trendy fashion, which in no time at all everyone else is copying. You don't always stick with your new ventures very long. You tend to move on to newer challenges, leaving others to consolidate and continue the project born of your initiating spark.

Your Unconscious Instincts You have strong urges to lead and to achieve. Most of your aims and actions stem from these unconscious instincts. Whether or not you always succeed in realizing your unconscious objectives is another matter, but as your basic orientation, you are seen as on a white charger, arm upraised, leading an army toward the successful storming of a previously unconquered fortress.

Aries children are rarely designated as underachievers; Aries adults tend to proceed with supreme self-confidence toward the top—in business, finance, creative arts, and the various professions. We are not guaranteeing that just because your unconscious instincts steer you toward upper-echelon success you are bound to make it, but onward and upward are the directions you naturally face, without even thinking about it. One of your other unconscious urges is to keep a weather eye out for bigger and better worlds to conquer. And you frequently spot one before you've really done justice to whatever project you're working on at the time. This can lead to a series of great starts and dwindled away follow-ups. Your basic urge to achieve is commendable, but how often have you enthusiastically hurled yourself into some fascinating new enterprise, only to lose interest after a bit and prance off, with equal enthusiasm, after a new objective? Because unconscious instincts *can* be modified (or improved upon) by a conscious act of the will—and the Aries will is really powerful—it might behoove you to buttress that great urge for achievement with the purposeful completion of projects you so dynamically begin.

Your unconscious urge to lead gives you what are known as executive abilities. You take the comprehensive view of a matter, delegate tasks as appropriate to others, and are the decision maker par excellence in a group situation. You quite naturally take over the reins of leadership; usually, other people quite naturally expect you to do so. Where there is a leader, there are followers, and you have a special gift for arousing the enthusiasm of others to participate in pursuing whatever goal you have set your sights on. This particular quality, which is actually a sort of magnetism, can make you a world leader, a political chieftain, a social arbiter—or the bellwether of your own little group. Bellwether, incidentally (being a male sheep, wearing a bell, usually the leader of the flock), is an apt tag for Aries, the sign of the Ram.

Your unconscious drives to achieve and to lead are also the basis for your competitive spirit. As a matter of fact you unconsciously welcome competition, for it sparks off a challenge without which achievement and leadership would be somewhat empty objectives. Fundamentally, your quest is for the prize.

Your unconscious instincts are operative at all times, asleep or awake. They are part of your totality. However, by far the greatest number of your dreams stem from . . .

Your Subconscious Desires Subconsciously, you wish to impose your will on others. This is a logical follow-up to your unconscious instincts to lead and to achieve. It is evident during your waking hours in your aggressive manner of going after what you want, of overcoming obstacles and/or resistance from others. While you do not have the subconscious desire to hurt, you do subconsciously disregard the fact that others can be hurt by your aggressive pursuit of objectives. "You can't make an omelette without breaking a few eggs" is the motto of your subconscious.

Idealistic principles appeal to your subconscious. You might not verbalize it in so many words, but you do have a subconscious response to idealism and humanitarianism. There's a touch of the hero (or heroine) in every Aries person. The fireman who rushes into a burning building to save a life, the surgeon who blends skill and daring in an innovative operation, the soldier who risks his own life to save a comrade, are all Aries types. Though not all careers or events produce situations where such Arien extremes are possible, you do have the subconscious desire to perform outstanding feats, not only to distinguish yourself, but to help your fellow man. This quality may seem to be at variance with that previously mentioned disregard of incurring hurt to others as you pursue your objectives, but it's really a matter of perspective. If you were that fireman rushing into a burning building to save a life, you would indeed disregard any curious onlookers you happened to knock down on the way. Your first priority would be the rescue—the knocked-down onlookers merely the "few eggs" that got broken. Figuratively, this is your approach to life and your subconscious desires and motives operate accordingly.

In your dreams, whether they are of seemingly unimportant, everyday matters, or have a specific plot structure, your subconscious desires are being revealed. Invariably, there will be a particular desire involved, even though dream symbolism may cloud it, or distracting side issues may appear to predominate. You are not an aimless person in your waking hours, therefore you do not dream aimless dreams. Since you are also basically honest and straightforward (deviousness plays no part in the straight-to-the-point Aries nature), it is rather unlikely that you will have to delve through layer after layer of camouflage to arrive at the point of your dreams. A little camouflage, yes, but it is easily discernible. An example is the sort of dream where another individual in the dream is misbehaving, or being punished for a trait or act that is one of *your* failings. That would be your subconscious transferring the guilt—the subconscious urge for self-protection making you the onlooker rather than the culprit. This sort of thing you can spot in a minute through objective self-analysis. In general, because of your particular temperament, subconscious desires, and motives, your dreams will point out to you your need to develop certain qualities (patience, perhaps, as in a frustration dream) or may compensate for a current problem in your life, such as in an escape dream. Because one of your strongest subconscious desires is to impose your will on others, your dreams may be of situations in which various people are accepting—or thwarting—that objective. By understanding your subconscious desires, their basic slant and motivation—and understanding your unconscious instincts as well—you will be better able to identify the real meaning of your dream episodes.

Your Special Abilities and Talents These lie in the realm of your conscious state, the awareness and perception of your waking hours. Therefore, you should be consciously aware of your decisiveness, strong will, and aggressiveness—and you probably are. These qualities show up in your ability to make split-second judgments and decisions and your subsequent quick follow-up on matters about which you have been decisive. This is not to say that your decisions and follow-ups are necessarily correct and to your advantage, but merely that you have the ability to be positive and affirmative and to get things done. These, of course, can be splendid traits provided they are backed by a real understanding of the issues involved and directed toward constructive goals. Negatively, the same traits can impel you to go off on tangents, to leap before looking: decisive, but unwise. Take a moment to look back on your life to date. If it has been strewn here and there with a few unforgettable occasions where you leaped before first checking out where you'd be apt to land, hopefully you've learned from those experiences. Like the time when you fell madly in love and plunged into the relationship before noticing certain incompatibilities, basic differences in temperament and values; or the rather promising job you quit on impulse, only to find that you'd done yourself out of a nice seasonal bonus; or signing up for an extended educational course, in which you lost interest and were out the tuition fees. If you're a typical Arien, you'll probably find a few such examples. And it's doubtful that you'll need any subconscious reminders, via dreams, to learn from such experiences; your good, sound *conscious* realization that overimpulsiveness or impatience can work against your best interests ought to provide the impetus for using a bit more foresight in your dynamic progress.

There is a potent generative force associated with Aries. This stems from its position as the first sign of the Zodiac and its cardinal and fire qualities. Symbolically, Aries is the prime force, the generative power of creation. Translated into a workable description of you as an Aries, this simply means that you have creative talents in which are blended originality, innovation, individualistic expression. This can pertain to the arts—painting, sculpting, writing, composing, designing—but can equally apply to creative thinking in business or finance, or in a profession such as law, education, medicine, science.

Your strong will shows up in many and diverse

ways, including your leadership and executive abilities. In any group of people, the majority tend to look about for one to take the lead (it is extremely rare to find a dozen or so individuals in a group, who are all leaders!). From any such group, a leader emerges, and you fit this role by natural qualification. We are speaking here of your abilities and talents—decisiveness, strong will, aggressiveness —not how you subsequently use them (for all we know, you might lead this theoretical group into jail, exile, or worse; then again, you might lead them to safety and salvation). But the important point here is that you should aim for a job, career, or life style in which your special qualities can be utilized constructively. If you are a square peg in a round hole, which, for an Arien, would mean a job with no challenge or potential for advancement, or a solitary kind of private life, with none to follow where you lead, not only should you make every effort to change your life pattern, but your dreams are undoubtedly telling you just that.

Both astrology and your dreams are guides in your life, signposts along the way, that inform you of what turnings to take, when to speed up, when to slow down, when a detour is advisable. When you know your destination—and if you are a typical Arien, you should have no doubts—self-understanding through astrology and its correlation with your dreams can give you a head start. Incidentally, that phrase "head start" is particularly Arien; for not only does Aries rule the head (each sign of the Zodiac relates to a part of the human body), but the more you use your head—in the sense of exercising your keen, perceptive mind—the more you can make your life that glorious adventure you envision it to be. So if your life does not provide the opportunities for you to utilize your special abilities and talents, express that Arien initiative by creating opportunities for yourself. For example, if you're in an unsatisfactory job, explore the potential in other lines of work. Perhaps you could take a short course to develop a particular skill that will increase your value to an employer. But remember, basically you are a leader, not a follower, so do work toward the ultimate goal of having your own business or profession. If your personal life is dull, become involved with stimulating groups—civic, political, academic, sporting. Or maybe a relationship is unproductive, and it's time to either revamp its pattern or call it quits. A really healthy relationship inspires you to do your best and to be your best; a relationship that brings worry, turmoil, stress, is counter-productive and not at all the Aries style. Your dreams are not only reflecting your current problems, but are also providing clues to solutions, so be on the watch for them.

How Do You Dream? This doesn't refer to the position in which you sleep, but rather to the quality, consistency, and subject matter of your nightly excursions into the dream state. In all probability, your dreams reflect your general temperament by being action dreams, in which you cover a good deal of territory in one night's dream episodes. You might also tend to have numerous, unconnected dream experiences in one sleep period—particularly if you have the Aries failing of starting many projects without too clear a picture of their eventual outcome.

Frustration and/or confinement dreams are rather typical Arien dreams, as well, for any ordinary day produces quite a few situations where people or objects do not move as rapidly as you desire. Your subconscious may be telling you to slow down, to have a bit more patience, when it crowds your night with a series of dream frustrations, and, to establish clearer perspective and priority in your waking hours.

Unless you have a physical or emotional problem that causes you to be an insomniac, your natural way is to plunge headlong into the dream route, to be asleep as soon as your head hits the pillow. This is also an expression of your overall eagerness to get on with the matter at hand. Maybe, too, your subconscious is eager to get its messages across! You tend to have physical action dreams, which are echoed in your many body movements through the night.

What Specific Dream Categories Mean to You

Confinement Dreams Surely these are some of the most distressing dreams for a free-wheeling Arien! In this sort of dream, the confinement may be represented in a physical way. You may be in a locked room, or a dead-end corridor, or one of those vague places, so popular in the dream world, where you don't know exactly where you are but you do know you can't get out. Then there is the confinement of circumstances, in which you go over and over in your mind the various possible ways out of a binding situation, only to realize you're boxed in no matter what you do. This type of dream usually represents a waking-state event, most often one that has already occurred in the recent past, and about which you have some feeling of guilt. You cannot find the outlet or solution because the deed is done, but your subconscious keeps reminding you of it nevertheless. If this is a one-shot type of dream, it may be that your subconscious has received a slight seep through from your conscience. If this type of dream is fairly frequent (though the environments may differ, your feeling of confinement persists), then it's likely that there is a way to make amends, restitution, or whatever for the incident about which you feel guilty. Try to remember the details of the dream, as a clue will be provided via a person in your dream, or a seemingly unconnected remark, or an intuition. Yes, you can have intuition within a dream.

Insecurity Dreams The most popular dreams of all! Since our waking hours are beset by various worries, apprehensions, and, particularly, the need for a sense of security, many of these dreams are carry-overs from the conscious to the subconscious state. Invariably you dream that something is lost; not being able to find your pocketbook or wallet is, quite obviously, a reference to material security. Or you dream you've forgotten something vital; or you're suddenly stranded in a strange place with no transportation, no money, and no friends. Dreams of that sort usually find you awakening with a feeling of apprehension, vaguely defined as the dream slips away into the recesses of your memory. Unless this type of dream is decidedly similar and frequent in which case there is probably a major security problem in your waking hours (material or emotional), don't worry too much about it. No one enjoys feeling insecure, an Arien least of all. If you are consciously, in your waking state, using all the Arien force and drive to combat insecurity, in whatever area it exists, you will ultimately resolve the problem. If, on the other hand, you are lazy and have not as yet plumbed in depth your potential to achieve the material or emotional security you crave, then your subconscious is prodding you with these dreams in order to get you moving.

Frustration Dreams Frustration dreams are rather similar to insecurity and confinement dreams, with one important difference. In the latter two categories, you feel unable to cope with a situation or event that "somehow" came upon you. This actually represents a bit of self-doubt (unusual for an Aries, but possible). In the frustration dream, you have done your best to ensure that an event takes place or a project is accomplished—and then there comes along some circumstance or person who frustrates *you.* The old familiar impatience and anger rise, even in the dream, as you are unable to batter your way through to the desired goal, whatever it may be. You tend to awaken feeling very irritable after such a dream. Usually you can identify in your dream the person who, in your waking hours, is blocking you. If it is your boss, an authority figure in your dream will step in and harass you (parent, teacher, traffic cop, and so on); or if it is your mate, then the individual in your dream will be a relationship figure (maybe even someone out of the past, whom you once loved). This type of dream is significant because it does help you to identify the real source of your frustration—which it is entirely possible you have not faced up to. Once recognized, your flare for taking decisive action toward finding the solution can bring the matter out of the subconscious and into your conscious life, whereupon there will be no need for such a dream.

Passive Dreams Strange for you to be an onlooker instead of a participant! In this type of dream, though, your subconscious which may not get the chance to express itself via the reflective, meditative process during your waking hours takes over and propels you over to the sidelines so that you get a more comprehensive picture of what's really going on in your life. This is the sort of dream where you are observing the action as though it were on a movie or TV screen. It may comprise any sort of subject matter, but in your dream you are not at all personally involved. You do not experience emotion or reaction, but merely observe in total detachment. Your subconscious is literally showing you the overall view, and if upon waking you ponder the events or people portrayed in this dream episode, you will find that they relate to a current situation in your life. You've got a good, healthy ego and there's nothing wrong with that; but it could be compared to one actor in a stage play, intent on his own lines, moves, and cues, not overly aware of other performers and their importance to the main plot. In this dream, you are the producer and the audience, passively observing the whole production. Your own cue from this type of dream is to learn to step aside from yourself so that you get a better perspective on the situation suggested by this dream. Any extra emphasis on an apparently unimportant person or incident should be carefully evaluated as well. There could be a detail you've overlooked in the waking-life corollary to the dream episode, whereby the key to the matter will become apparent.

Action Dreams As an Arien, you are especially prone to action dreams—the kind of dream in which you actually seem to experience the feeling of motion, the flexing of your muscles, or perhaps the passage through space or even time. Sometimes the action in your dream bridges over into physical impulses in your sleeping body, and as you catapult yourself into the waking state you find you are already sitting up, with one foot on the floor, or perhaps you are on your feet and crossing the room as you awaken. There is usually a sense of urgency associated with action dreams, which are different from the dreams in which you *observe* yourself in action, or in which your actions seem but a fragment of the total you. In fact, in this very real sort of action dream, particularly when it carries over into the waking state, your subconscious is pretty close to meshing with your conscious life. Because the majority of all dreams do tend to be clothed in symbolism, the actions you perform in this type of dream are not necessarily duplicates of waking-life situations, though they are quite close. For example, you may dream that you are hurrying to keep an appointment, perhaps getting into your car and actually feeling the wheel beneath your hands; or you are trying to overtake someone whose head start places him or her some distance ahead of you, and you quicken your pace and begin to run. The sense of urgency and the impulse to take physical action in order to keep the appointment, overtake the person, or whatever relates to a correspondingly urgent matter in your waking life (a major sales campaign, for instance, or a vital contact you wish to make). This matter may require mental action, or it may involve a decision concerning a relationship, or perhaps a career project on which you are very eager to begin work. Because you are an Aries, your subconscious translates this into dynamic physical action (so dynamic that it whirls right into your waking moments) and usually with a vital feeling of haste involved. In such dreams, you rarely ever experience the culmination of whatever you've been physically rushing to do, but this does not make it a frustration dream. Your subconscious is actually setting the stage for a most productive day to follow—getting you in the mood, so to speak, to get out there and do things.

Recurring Dreams Your subconscious is patiently trying to get a message across to you—why won't you see it? Recurring dreams do not have to be exact repeats of prior dreams (though once in a while they are), but are very similar as to situation, theme, and your own reactions in the dream. Usually, this sort of dream generates a déjà-vu feeling—a sense that you have many times experienced this familiar, unfolding plot. Such a dream is extremely significant and you should do your best to recall all details and to relate the dream to a waking-life situation. It may refer to a debt you owe (moral, emotional, or spiritual indebtedness is more likely than financial) or something you've not done which you should do. This may even apply to a neglected opportunity or failure to develop a special talent or it may relate to a confrontation you've been avoiding. Think deeply on your recurring dreams, for they represent something that must be worked out, settled, or initiated. Also under this category is the *resumed dream,* which is of equal and vital importance. This occurs when you are awakened for some reason or other, are fully aware of the waking state, then fall asleep again and pick up a dream just where you left off. Your subconscious is drumming a point across to you and no interruption is going to interfere.

Escape Dreams You'll tend to have this sort of dream mostly when your everyday life is not in accord with your talents and temperament. A humdrum routine, where there's little opportunity for excitement or adventure, can prompt your subconscious to pamper you a bit with dreams of taking off into the blue, leaping over a wall, leaving a room and slamming the door, running for a train, or any other form of locomotion (it's the act of moving away from where you are that's significant). You may even dream of sleeping as a form of escape (confusing, isn't it?), though Ariens are unlikely to seek, even in their subconscious, this passive form of escape, unless very fatigued. Escape dreams, if not accompanied by unpleasant factors (fear, apprehension, nervousness) represent your subconscious opening the safety valve a bit. If you can't escape waking restrictions, then at least you can have the dream pleasure of doing so. If such dreams are accompanied by fear or apprehension, such as someone chasing you with vaguely evil intent, the message is somewhat different for it would represent your subconscious worry that a transgression of yours will be found out and punished or that you are seeking to evade an additional responsibility. However, the pleasanter type of escape dream, in which you relish the flight from the here and now, can also mean your subconscious is urging you to take the necessary steps to change whatever situation in your life is producing the need for such dreams of escape.

Sex Dreams Whether your sex dreams involve a partner (invariably a total stranger to you in the dream) or are self-induced sexual dream episodes, the message from your subconscious almost always ties in with your sex drive and the activity and quality of your sex life in waking hours. If you have a rewarding sex life, sex dreams are infrequent. If your sex life is unsatisfactory or inactive, then this vital drive is somewhat repressed, pushed back into your subconscious, and shows up in your dreams. For Ariens especially—and for Arien males in particular—other factors also contribute to sex dreams. When Ariens are frustrated in their pursuit of a major goal—usually related to career, money, or status (the achievement syndrome)—the males can become temporarily impotent, the females entirely uninterested in sex. Under such conditions, your sex drive, having retreated to your subconscious, will not be totally denied and so is expressed in dream episodes. Accordingly, you will find that as you progress in your pursuit of whatever goal is dominant in your life, your waking-hours sex drive increases and, assuming it finds a healthy outlet, will not lurk about in your dreams!

Sensuous Dreams Sensuous dreams involve the five senses: sight, smell, hearing, taste, and touch. Sex is not involved in the sensuous dream, except as an occasional by-product. In this sort of dream you actually *feel* the function of the sense in question. The taste of the food is very real, the sound is remarkably audible, the scent is specific and identifiable, the object viewed is sharply outlined or brilliantly hued, or the object touched is as bulky or textured as in waking hours. In most other dreams, there is some vagueness, a subtle sense of unreality, or of participating with any of the senses in a veiled way. In the sensuous dream, things are as real as in everyday life. Your senses of sight, smell, and hearing are somewhat accentuated, symbolically, as Aries rules the head. Symbolically, too, a dream in which you view (with the special clarity that marks the sensuous dream) a particular object, pattern, scene, or person has significance in terms of *mental* clarity. You see (realize) with new awareness a situation or event in your waking life to which you should make every effort to correlate this dream. The same with a dream in which you hear, with extra sharpness, a sound or a person's voice. Your subconscious is clearing away the shadows, enabling you to see with your mind's eye, to hear with added comprehension, a specific message that will help you in your waking hours. A sensuous dream involving your sense of smell, taste, or touch would relate to sense pleasures in your everyday life (the need for them or the lack of them, as the case may be). If the odor or taste is unpleasant or the object touched is abrasive or hurtful, this is your subconscious cautioning you not to overindulge in that sensual area where you are prone to excess.

Precognitive Dreams This is the sort of dream that is a forerunner to an actual event. Sometimes the dream event and the following real-life event are identical; sometimes the theme of the two is the same, and though the details differ, you recognize the link between the episode and the actuality. Dreams like this can give you a spooky feeling if you are not particularly interested in occult matters, or if you tend to shy away from anything other-worldly. As a matter of fact, Ariens are not as subject to the precognitive dream as are individuals of some other signs, though when you do have such a dream, the later events prove that the dream was indeed clear-cut, easily recognizable as the forerunner to the event. In the precognitive dream, your subconscious is running ahead of you, temporarily out of the bonds of time and space. The value of this sort of dream is that it might prepare you for the later event; but as it is very rare that an individual recognizes a precognitive dream until subsequent developments identify it as such, this value is rather nebulous. It does point up the fact, however, that it is good to keep track of your dreams, analyzing them with the view that once in a while they could be precognitive.

Peopled Dreams As an Aries, you tend to dream about lots of people, but they are often not too clear as to features or other details of appearance. This ties in with your own self-focus and your involvement with comprehensive plans. You tend to see people as a crowd rather than as individuals. Accordingly, in your dreams people are apt to be background material—props to the production you're staging. This is natural enough for an Arien, although your subconscious is undoubtedly providing you with some clues, here and there, concerning a specific individual who may stand out for a special reason among the somewhat casual array of your dream population. A certain action, facial expression, or remark made by a person in your dream could be significant, especially if it seems to be out of context with the general theme of the dream.

Symbols in Dreams Although there is a lot of general symbolism in dreams, specific objects can stand out with special meaning once in a while in a dream episode. The elements—fire, earth, air, and water—correlate to spirit, matter, mind, and emotion, respectively. Of these the element of fire is particularly meaningful to those born in the fire sign, Aries. Fire also represents spiritual awakening; a dream of fire that included feelings of danger would be your subconscious pointing up your need for increased spiritual awareness. On the other hand, fire under control (such as in a warm and welcoming fireplace scene) would denote harmony between your spiritual principles and your general approach to life. A dream involving the element of air (flying, reveling in the fresh air of a country meadow, gazing at the night sky, and so on) signifies your potential for mental expansion. Air-related and fire-related dreams, unless acutely unpleasant, are compatible with your temperament, and show that your subconscious is urging you on to develop your full spiritual and mental potential. Other symbols in dreams can be animals, numbers, colors, abstract designs, and so on. If you should dream of the number one, the color red, or a four-footed horned animal (all super-Arien), that dream will be quite meaningful. Your subconscious is pinpointing, through symbolism, your real identity, even your mission in life, so be especially aware of all the details of such a dream.

Chapter 5

Taurus
(April 21–May 21)

Your unconscious state is the source of your natural instincts, while your subconscious is the realm of your innermost desires. Your Sun sign represents your own unique individuality. Because you are a Taurean, your dreams reflect this individuality and reveal your own special unconscious and subconscious states.

TAURUS is an Earth sign, ruled by Venus, fixed in quality (which means stable and steady). The blend of earthiness and fixity in your Sun sign is apparent in your temperament, for you are determined, practical, persevering, usually patient, and not subject to flightiness or indecision. Your pleasant, easygoing disposition reflects the charm that's associated with the planet Venus, as does your love of comfort and your affectionate nature. Astrology very often uses quite literal terminology. That Earth-sign quality shows up in your affinity to growing things of the earth (Taureans are noted for having a "green thumb" and the most lushly luxuriant gardens in their neighborhoods) as well as your inclination toward owning property. Taurus is the builder of the Zodiac, and whether you are actually involved in any aspect of the construction business (for which you'd have a decided flair) or express this talent through building a solid, strongly based career in another field, your orientation is toward establishing firm bases and carefully building the superstructure with precision and patience. The Earth orientation is also evident in your sense of material values. Money is another of your natural environments—as in a career in a money field such as banking, investments, or loan companies, or by automatically becoming treasurer of any organization to which you belong, or in handling the family budget in such a way that best buys are a way of life and resources are watchfully nurtured.

Your Unconscious Instincts You have strong urges to sustain and perpetuate. Many of your actions and objectives stem from these unconscious instincts. The sequence of zodiacal signs is interesting from the standpoint of how each follows up on its preceding sign. Whereas Aries, your preceding sign, initiates the action, innovates the ideas and plans, and then is frequently off to newer challenges, Taurus takes over that newborn material and builds of it a splendid enterprise. No task is too great and no hours too long for you to spend on—what is to you—the supremely satisfying act of perpetuating a worthwhile project. You are very much concerned with long-range goals, long-term plans. As a matter of fact, if things progress at too rapid a pace, you can become a bit uneasy. You are most comfortable when sustaining the kind of work load that is not at all burdensome when it produces solid results. When those results flourish into permanence and stability, and especially when there are tangible, material rewards, you are literally in your element.

This urge to sustain is evident in your relationships as well, for you are the one to whom others turn when they need to feel a sense of security. You are the one who is *there* when needed. Because you are seldom in doubt about your own opinions or convictions, you generate this certainty to others, sustaining them in their hour of need like a tower of strength. These subconscious urges to sustain and to perpetuate are innate in you, your automatic response to many a situation in your life. Of course, how you direct your unconscious urges is up to you; the material is there not only for great accomplishments but for contributing to the happiness of others. On the other hand, it can be used negatively—in which case that admirable urge to perpetuate can degenerate into mere stubbornness, i.e., there are only two ways of doing a thing, your way and the wrong way, and things are going to be done your way now and forever. Or that fine and comforting urge to sustain can be negatively polarized through possessiveness. You are not only going to be there when needed, you are going to take over the other individual's life lock, stock, and barrel!

In a material way, your urges to sustain and perpetuate can make you a successful business person, as you hang on to your initial investment and perpetuate it into a going concern (a financial empire, even). Or you can make life miserable for everyone around you in your eternal quest to save a penny—an extreme example, but possible. Unconscious instincts can be recognized, nurtured, and directed into positive expression by an act of the conscious will. These instincts are constantly operative, asleep or awake, forming a backdrop to your dreams. However the majority of your dreams are produced by . . .

Your Subconscious Desires Subconsciously, you wish to hold on to what you have and, if possible, add to it. That is the natural follow-up on your unconscious instincts to sustain and to perpetuate. This is apparent in your waking hours by the way in which you care for and guard your possessions, whether these are material objects or individuals who are important in your life. In the case of material possessions, you derive a certain satisfaction from enhancing your home, such as keeping the silver brightly polished, neatly stacking up those piles of linen or cases of canned goods (having obtained them at a sale in which quality merchandise was offered at half-price!). Because you are given to long-range planning, you aren't too concerned about fads in clothing, housewares, or life style; you're building for the future and your possessions are usually of a classic timelessness.

In the area of personal relationships, your subconscious wish to hold on to what you have, and to add to it, reflects in that trait we mentioned previously —possessiveness—which, if not overdone, can be both flattering and comforting provided the individuals in question are not ultra freedom-oriented, in which case there may be a problem. You tend to ensure the continuance of a relationship and to deepen the bonds by establishing regular and secure routines. This includes the friend you go to the movies with every Friday night or those people you visit every other Sunday, or that lover in whom you have established an eagerness for your Tuesdays, Thursdays, and Saturdays together.

In the area of your job, career, and finances, your subconscious wish to hold on to what you have and to add to it, prompts you to affiliate yourself with a company that is solid, secure, with the maximum of fringe and retirement benefits (that's you, looking to the future). Also, you look for a firm in which hard work, attention to details, and dependableness will be rewarded by regular advancements and raises. Although you would hardly turn it down if it were offered to you, overnight success is not usually your main goal. You are nothing if not realistic and you get a special satisfaction from the fruits of your extended labors.

In your dreams, whether they are vague or definite, your subconscious desires are being revealed. Usually there is a specific desire involved, even though symbolic figures or apparently meaningless distractions may be included. Because you are a person who is innately sure of yourself and your opinions, in whom certainty and security play a large part in your life, events or situations in your waking hours that produce *un*certainty or *in*security tend to throw you very much off balance (more so than the same condition would affect people of other signs). This would show up in your dreams in a disturbing way, as you struggle through the nights with frustration dreams, confinement or insecurity dreams, and so on. Your dreams will tend, in general, to be uncomplicated and to deal with specific matters however unrelated they may appear to be to waking-hours events. Your subconscious will accent your wish to hold on to your possessions: You're a natural for the insecurity dream where you've lost your purse or wallet! Your subconscious can also provide you with alternatives—and in this way can teach you to be less singleminded in your view of a certain matter. A dream in which you are faced with choice or selection, even if the objects in question are entirely unimportant, will be significant in terms of letting you know there's more than one way to accomplish a purpose. By being aware of your subconscious desires and conscious instincts, you will be in a better position to translate the real meaning of your dream episodes.

Your Special Abilities and Talents These are in the area of your conscious state, your waking-hours awareness. You are indeed probably conscious of many of your special talents such as your ability to be practical, even in the face of distractions and side issues; your ability to endure, which shows up in your patience under stress; your acceptance of responsibility and faithful fulfillment of same; and your ability to maintain conservative, established practices, even when those around you are pushing for trendy changes. Your loyalty should also come under the category of ability, for not everyone can remain loyal to an individual or a principle when either is under fire. Regarding your talents, there is the previously mentioned flair for handling funds of your own or others, but you also have a talent in what could be broadly defined as artistic expression: possibly painting, sculpting, design, handiwork, or music. Taurus rules the throat and many Taureans have beautiful singing voices. Venus, your sign ruler, does give you a special affinity with the arts, music, and cultural matters in general. Then there is your talent for things of the earth: gardening, mining, agriculture, real estate, architecture, urban or rural planning.

Your practicality shows up in a multitude of ways. In a group situation when others get carried away with subjective thinking or overemotionalism, yours is the voice of reason, pointing out the realistic facts of the matter and suggesting workable solutions. When "popular opinion" influences many an impressionable soul to climb on the latest bandwagon, you hold to tried-and-true principles. While you can be as ambitious or idealistic as anyone, your aims are based on practical values—on probables instead of possibles. In the area of humanitarian ideals, you tend toward feeding and housing people as the number-one priority, as opposed to high-flown rhetoric with no tangible action. If you are a truly positive and evolved Taurean, you also put your money where your mouth is! Your endurance is tremendous and can even work against you sometimes, when you put up for far too long with situations that really ought to be changed.

All of these abilities and talents can, of course, be either utilized or neglected. You do have a lazy streak and may be inclined to put off until tomorrow and tomorrow and tomorrow. This sort of thing is very likely to show up in your dreams, as you encounter people, events, or situations in your dreams which leave you with a nagging impression of something you ought to have done but did not do. You like your creature comforts and you do not like to be rushed, which could have been why you neglected that opportunity to join a lively group where you could have met good marriage prospects or made valuable business contacts. But no, you preferred to stay at home with your music, your midnight snacks, and your comfy recliner chair! Or perhaps you failed to look into an on-the-job opening that would lead to higher status, because you were reluctant to leave the familiar security of your everyday routine (there's such a thing as being too established, too conservative, too fixed). Think about your life to date, reflecting on some of those might-have-beens that are likely to pop up in your dreams. What your subconscious could be nudging you to do is to take any necessary steps to improve your life, in terms of your career or a relationship that brings out your best and utilizes your special talents.

Both astrology and dreams are aids in your realizing your potential. And "potential" is a word that should have meaning for you, inasmuch as your unconscious instincts to sustain and perpetuate and your subconscious desire to hold on to what you have and *add to it* lead to the future realization of the present promise. Be honest; are you really making the most of opportunities, or are you sort of drifting along—not doing badly, perhaps, but not exactly setting the world on fire. When Taurus really gets moving, there's no stopping the motion; it's getting started that is sometimes the problem. There's not much that can stand in the way of a charging bull, and as the Bull is the symbol of your sign, that's an appropriate statement. In case you're not making the most of your considerable potential, you'll pick up pointed reminders of this in your dreams from time to time, even though you may not recognize the correlation until you analyze them. The imagery of a Taurean sitting on a plush cushion and not bestirring himself or herself to take that first step out of the rut and into the mainstream just might fit you. You'll know if that image is you from the impression the majority of your dreams leave with you upon awakening. If you feel vaguely discontented, sluggish, or a bit apprehensive—but you're not sure about what—it's undoubtedly your subconscious prodding you to get off the dime.

How Do You Dream? It's a safe bet that from a physical standpoint your bed is an important item of furniture to you, providing the space and the comfort for you to squash yourself down into dreamland. But actually the question above has nothing to do with your sleeping environment. It's the quality and subject matter of your dreams we are talking about. In general, your dreams tend to have rather deep meanings, although until you (1) make a real effort to remember them, and (2) analyze them thoughtfully to find the correlation with real-life events, situations, or problems (past or present), you might not realize the important messages your subconscious is trying to get across to you. By making the firm resolve, just as you are falling asleep, that you *will* remember your dreams, you can train your conscious mind to receive the subconscious messages. This may not happen all at once, but persevere. You'll probably find that your dreams are fairly orderly, in the sense of having a beginning, a middle, and possibly an ending, although the vast majority of dreams do not have definite conclusions (this, because they invariably reflect unresolved conflicts or problems). You would also tend to have colorful dreams. The average person dreams in black and white, or muted tones of color, but you could very well be one of those creative people who dream in brilliant colors. You would also be prone to having an occasional precognitive dream, for earthy and practical as you are, you have a strong link with cosmic vibrations. Statistics show that Taureans lead the Zodiac in producing psychics. All of which make your dreams of more than passing importance, so be aware of them.

What Specific Dream Categories Mean to You

Confinement Dreams These dreams find you in places or situations from which you are unable to extricate yourself. You might have one of those physically confining dreams, where there's some vague danger threatening you, but you simply cannot move arms or legs even though you try with all your might. Or perhaps you are in a room without windows or doors, or have that Alice-in-Wonderland feeling as you encounter the same exit over and over again, only to find that it leads nowhere but to more of the same. While the feeling of being trapped is hardly a pleasant one, this dream episode is symbolic in the sense that its real-life corollary does not mean being trapped physically. This dream represents something that you have brought on yourself, very often an act of yours in the recent past in which you boxed yourself into a situation from which there is no apparent escape. This can refer to an unwise business deal or to an ultimatum situation in a relationship. There's a mixture of regret and guilt in this type of dream, for you are imprisoned by your own hand, so to speak. If you have repeated dream episodes of this nature, you should try to find a way to correct the matter in your waking hours, or at least to face up to it and get it into your conscious state as a matter that's over and done. Otherwise, your subconscious is apt to keep dredging it up in dreams.

Insecurity Dreams As security-minded as you are, this—the most widely experienced kind of dream—can be quite disturbing. In the insecurity dream, you're without something you need, or you've lost something vital, or you're simply lost. While no one relishes the dream of the lost money, tickets, car, or child—you, as a Taurean, suffer most of all! This sort of dream is likely to pop up when you have a waking-hours worry or fear, not full blown enough to occupy a chunk of your conscious mind (in which case you'd be less likely to dream of it), but tucked away in your subconscious, where it's apt to trot out in your nightly dreams to plague you under various guises. The actual fear or worry need not relate to the source of your fear or worry in the dream. Your dream of lost money could reflect your subconscious fear that you will "lose face" with your colleagues or neighbors if a certain event occurs. Or your dream of a lost child or pet may stem from subconscious apprehension about a love relationship that's begun to evidence disquieting symptoms. You may dream that you do not have all your clothes on, and though in such a dream other people in the dream rarely even notice your partial or complete exposure, still you are embarrassed and flustered. This represents an insecurity concerning something you've done (maybe a very trifling matter, actually) that you subconsciously fear will come to light and you'll be "exposed." Everyone has insecurity dreams from time to time, but if you have a lot of such dreams, your subconscious could be telling you you're a bit off-balance, in terms of putting too much importance on the value of money, possessions, or other material matters. An excessive number of insecurity dreams would spotlight your lack of faith, your need to balance more equitably the spiritual with the temporal.

Frustration Dreams This is the sort of dream where

your best-laid plans go astray and you are unable to complete what you set out to do. It may be a trip to the store or your office or to a friend's house, and suddenly you are prevented from continuing your progress, or you find yourself in a totally strange environment where there's no chance you'll be able to get where you were going. Whatever the content of the dream, it is the incompleted act that makes it a frustration dream. However, Taureans can take this type of dream in their stride. It is not quite so irritating to you as to people of some of the other signs. This is because you are not innately impatient, so if you cannot finish what you started during the dream episode, your subconscious philosophy of patience and perseverance comes to your rescue. You may pick up a clue in a frustration dream, however, as to an individual or situation in your waking hours that produces in you a feeling of frustration. It might be an associate to whom it is extremely difficult to project your ideas (and in the dream you've a message for someone but can't deliver it). Or perhaps the frustration stems from a love relationship where you subconsciously fear that your affection is not welcomed or appreciated, and you dream that your friend's house is empty when you finally get there. Your subconscious may be forcing you to face up to a frustrating situation you've refused to recognize in your waking hours.

Passive Dreams Really your cup of tea!—especially if you are a *lazy* Taurean. This is the sort of dream in which you make no effort at all. The picture unfolds before you and you watch with interest but with no decided emotions or reactions. When you see yourself in this kind of dream, it's as though the story were about someone else, not you at all. These can be the easiest dreams to remember, because in a sense you are observing and recording and are not distracted by participating in them. There will be clues or messages in this kind of dream, however, which could very well mean that your subconscious is spotlighting an incident or a person's motive which escaped you when you were actually part of the related event in the recent past. Although the subject matter of the dream is unlikely to match the real-life event, the essence will be there. Watching yourself go through your paces at a dreamed social function could be a sort of review of your actions in any other kind of group situation. Or, if the dream does not contain many people, but rather focuses on scenes, a nature panorama, and so on, this could relate to a decision you've made recently and how it is likely to affect your life style. The need to be objective is sometimes the message your subconscious projects through a passive dream, particularly when you correlate the dream with the real-life situation about which you tend to be subjective or overly emotional.

Action Dreams These dreams are identified by the physical activity that occurs in them. You may be running, walking, driving, and actually feeling your body or the vehicle in motion. Or you may be carrying something. As a Taurean you are especially prone to dreams of bearing burdens—whether it's a bag of groceries, an armful of books, or, like Atlas, the weight of the world on your shoulders. The action dream is different from those dreams in which you *see* yourself in action. In this dream you really seem to experience the bodily movements or whatever other physical effort is expended. The message from your subconscious is fairly simple to figure out, too. If the action in the dream is unpleasant—the burden too heavy, the walking fatiguing, or the effort of motion a strain—your subconscious is pointing out that the action you are taking in an actual situation is not in tune with your temperament. Alternatives may work better, so look for questions of choice or selection in your dream, even if it is something as simple as turning away from your intended route, or running after some individual in your dream, with a sense of urgency. Identifying that individual might be the key to your burden problem. Symbols often appear in dreams with regard to individuals: An older person (a father-mother authority figure) or a person to whom you are romantically attracted in your dream (representing a real-life relationship, not necessarily romantic, but one that is beneficial to you). Your action dreams may reflect a decision you have made within the past week or so; maybe after mulling over a question in your mind and floundering a bit in considering the pros and cons, you came to a definite conclusion involving some action you are going to take. The action dream can be preparing you to get moving on this.

Recurring Dreams This is the sort of dream in which the entire plot is familiar to you as it unfolds. It may be an exact repeat of a dream you've had more than once before, or the general tone of the dream is repetitive. Obviously, this relates to a matter that needs to be worked out, a problem that has to be dealt with sooner or later, or perhaps some sort of change in your inner direction that is still dormant in your conscious mind, but for which your subconscious is setting the opening scene. Try to remember all the details of a recurring dream, for there will be links to both past and present interests in your life. If you are a typical Taurean, you have a lot of intuition—maybe not so much perception. Your intuition enables you to know, almost instinctively, the answers to certain questions, or the right action to take at the right time. Perception, however, is a quick grasp of any given situation, in which the mind perceives multitudinous details, impressions, and subtleties, blending all of these together into an instant awareness of the real meaning of the situation. Since you tend to be rather concentrated in your thought processes, perception may be a bit lacking, and your subconscious is attempting, through the recurring dream, to get through to you some facts you've not perceived in your waking hours. Also under this category is the *resumed dream,* in which you are fully awakened for some reason or other, then upon going back to sleep resume the dream where it was cut off. This is a meaningful kind of dream as there is something in it that is vital for you to know, despite the break in the episode.

Escape Dreams This is the dream in which you leave some place or condition that is not so good, to enter a place or condition that is relaxed, enjoyable, and, most of all, free. You escape from the unpleasant into the pleasant, whether the dream takes the form of catching the next plane out, or escaping through an exit of some sort, or running out of the shadows into the sunshine. Obviously, there is some condition in your life from which you would like to escape and your subconscious is making that possible, if only in the dream state. There may sometimes be clues in this kind of dream as to how you can "escape" a real-life problem, but usually it represents merely your wish to do so. If you are beleaguered by problems in your waking hours, the escape dream has a therapeutic value as well, releasing through dreams some of the pressures in your daily life. You usually awaken refreshed from an escape dream; occasionally it can even put you in the frame of mind to find the solution to a waking-hours problem—a bit of psychological buildup from your subconscious!

Sex Dreams Taureans usually have a strong sex drive, so it is likely that you do experience a sex dream now and then. For the most part, individuals who have a satisfying sex life in their waking hours are not as prone to dreaming about sex as those who do not. The simplest interpretation of a dream in which sex is featured is that some repression of the sex drive in real life diverts it into dream experience. However, there can more to it than that, especially for a Taurean. An Earth sign, Venus-ruled, Taurus' natural attitude toward sex is wholesome, healthy, direct, and uncomplicated. When complications arise in your life (though they need not be sexual, but may relate to money, status, achievement), you are thrown a bit off balance and may subconsciously turn to the one area of your life of which you feel secure, seif-confident, vital. Therefore, your sex dream may be your subconscious reminding you that you are indeed a great guy or gal, well able to cope with those complications in other areas of your life. It is also possible that your partner in the sex dream may represent an individual for whom you have a supressed sexual attraction in real life. Or, this person in the dream may be the image of one who has aroused your latent sexual desire.

Sensuous Dreams To begin with, you Taureans are super sensuous. The sensuous dream does not relate to sex, except possibly in a peripheral way. The senses of sight, hearing, smell, taste, and touch are featured in the sensuous dream; for a Taurean, there's an extra emphasis on taste and touch. Even in your waking hours, you are quite a "feeler." You are the one who squeezes the melons, who examines the dress or suit material with tactile thoroughness, who strokes and caresses your dear ones with many a love pat. You are affectionate, and you display this by various gentle and tender touches. As to your sense of taste, you must admit you do enjoy your food. Therefore, in your sensuous dreams you are most likely to be feeling or tasting something, and the chief characteristic of doing these in a sensuous dream is that the sense impression is so vivid, so realistic, that it seems to be exactly like doing the same thing in real life. However, there is no vague feeling of unreality that is present in many other dreams. If your sensuous dream is pleasant, it is simply the basic, Taurean, *you*, enjoying sense pleasures in dreamland as well as in your waking hours—your subconscious fulfilling your wish for this sort of satisfaction. If the dream is unpleasant (you might experience a feeling of nausea as you eat and eat and eat, or you may touch an abrasive substance that hurts), then your subconscious is advising you to hold a tighter rein on your appetites.

Precognitive Dreams This sort of dream may be explicit—when an event or situation you dream about actually "comes true" in every detail in the immediate future; or it may be the impression the dream leaves with you that is verified shortly thereafter by an event producing the same reactions as did the dream. Not everyone has precognitive dreams, but Taureans tend to experience them. Despite the fact that you are noted for your down-to-earth practicality and your no-nonsense attitude toward many otherworldly subjects, you have a deep, instinctive cosmic awareness and are somehow tuned in to that beyond-time-and-space realm, in which the past, present, and future can be viewed as a continuing stream of consciousness. So, you may indeed have a precognitive dream now and then and, strangely enough, you could be among the few who recognize the precognitive dream for what it is. (Most people realize their dreams were precognitive only when verified by later events.) Since it's possible for you to have the advantage of this advance knowledge, we do not need to remind you to pay attention to all details of a precognitive dream, as you can gain valuable insight into future happenings.

Peopled Dreams The people in your dreams may be an array of strangers, passing across the screen of your nightly viewing, or they may be specific individuals whom you know now or have known in the past. But a person in your dream may not be the person he or she seems to be. That sounds confusing, but very often your subconscious drives a point home with imagery; that girl or boy you dream about may be a projection of yourself, or the total stranger who challenges you in some way could be an individual you've recently met and instinctively disliked, even though the dream person bears no resemblance to the real person. Groups or crowds of people may represent a certain condition in your life. If you're pushing through a crowd, it is an expression of your competitive spirit or if the crowd is going in the opposite direction from you, hindering your progress, this can mean a struggle you're involved in during waking hours, to achieve a career goal or a social objective. Many strange faces floating through your dreams represent your concern about the impression you are making on others; if they are pleasant faces, no need to worry for you're making the desired impression and your subconscious is telling you so. If they are scowling faces, there may be need for improvement in some facet of your personality expression, and your subconscious is telling you that too. As a Taurean, you have a healthy regard for relationships, being neither too self-reliant nor too dependent on others. The people in your dreams, therefore, are probably a mixture of pleasant and unpleasant people as in real life. You can pick up clues from their various attitudes or comments to correlate these dreams with current interests.

Symbols in Dreams There is a lot of general symbolism in dreams, such as the previously mentioned episodes in which an individual represents an image or figure, but once in a while you will dream of something that is particularly symbolic—perhaps an animal, color, number, abstract design or pattern, or an element such as fire, earth, air, or water. The elements are astrologically meaningful, of course, as fire represents the spirit; earth, the material body; air, the mind; and water, the emotions. The element of earth is especially significant for you, as yours is an Earth sign. A pleasant dream involving earthy matters (gardening, fruits of the earth, scenes featuring meadows, mountains, trees, and so on) is a reaffirmation of some of your basic ideals and principles, and perhaps a reminder from your subconscious to hang on to them. Earth- and water-related dreams are compatible with your temperament and show that your subconscious is urging you on to develop your full potential. Dreaming of an animal will be symbolic insofar as it emphasizes what the animal means to *you.* If you like domestic animals, for example, dreaming of a dog, cat or hamster can be dreaming of a love object. If you don't like the little creatures, dreaming of one can mean you're uneasy about the motives of someone you know. If you should dream of the number three, the color green, or of a bull or cow (whether you like the beast or not, the Bull is your symbol), that dream will be significant. Your subconscious is spotlighting through symbolism your true identity, even your life goals, so unravel the symbolism to obtain the inner meaning of this dream.

Chapter 6

Gemini
(May 22–June 21)

Your natural instincts flow from your unconscious, your deepest desires are found in your subconscious. Your Sun sign spotlights your own unique individuality. Because you are a Gemini, your dreams express both your unconscious instincts and subconscious desires in specifically Gemini fashion.

GEMINI is an air sign, ruled by Mercury, mutable in quality (which means adaptable). The element of air, the mobility of Mercury, and that adaptability signified by the mutable quality, blend to make you a lively, restless, inquisitive person, with a quick wit and multiple interests. Never a dull moment when there's a Gemini around. You're a great conversationalist and like to be physically on the move here, there, and everywhere. A job or life style where you are shut off from others, or have to sit in the same place for hours on end, is decidedly *not* for you. Your facile mind enables you to learn almost anything quickly and easily. How long you retain what you've learned is another matter, but usually it's long enough to pass that exam or get a special job which requires just the knowledge you have, at least temporarily, on tap. You make friends easily, and in friendship, as in practically all your interests, variety is the spice of life for you. Your flair with words equips you excellently for a career in some area of the communications field: writing, teaching, selling, acting, news dissemination—any career where you are transmitting ideas or information to others. That air-Mercury-mutable blend can, however, also cut into your power of concentration. You've a short attention span and tend to skim superficially over the surface of things, which often serves your purpose very well but can prevent you, sometimes, from making the most of your great potential.

Your Unconscious Instincts You have strong urges to communicate and to associate. Associate, in this sense, means not only to associate with other individuals (many Gemini people dislike being alone and seek to be in the company of others as often as possible) but also to associate words, meanings, theories, ideas, one to the other. Because you are an air-sign person, your basic slant is toward mental activity. This does not mean that you're without emotions or physical urges, but just about everything you do—all your interests and goals—are first sifted through your mind and the analytical process. Added to the air element, the Mercurial temperament, and the mutability of your sign, is the sign's symbol: the Twins, the influence of duality. All of this contributes to the many facets to your nature and personality, and forms a part of your unconscious instincts as well. Your urge to associate with others stems very much from this Twins symbolism; it is often said that Gemini is ever seeking its other twin and to this purpose searches out new associations, experimental relationships.

Your urge to communicate finds expression in your conversational fluency, your delight in spreading news, and in general your flair for working with words. On a social level, this adds to your popularity and your ease in relating with other people. You can always find some common interest to discuss with even the shyest member of a group. In terms of a career, your urge to communicate makes you a natural in the fields of advertising or news media. If you are a positive, evolved Gemini, with humanitarian instincts as well, your urge to communicate can make you an ideal person to bridge the communications gap between opposing groups, even on a global scale. Words are the tools of communication and you are naturally and unconsciously equipped to play your role in the world of words.

Negatively, your urges to communicate and associate prompt you to flit about constantly, never staying long enough in one place to form meaningful associations or to communicate significantly. This is negative only in the sense that you are not getting deeply enough beneath the surface of anything, even beneath the surface of yourself, to discover what you really are and where you're going. For the most part, you have good intentions, and your adaptability enables you to be diplomatic, tactful, and to "get around" a situation without making too many waves. And your ability to communicate also makes it possible for you to talk your way out of many a sticky situation!

Your unconscious urges to communicate and to associate lead you toward a life style in which other people are very much involved. Although the realm of the mind is your natural habitat, you are drawn toward expressing abstract ideas in a humanistic framework. These unconscious instincts are always operative, whether you are awake or asleep, and form an overall basis of your dreams. However, the greater portion of your dreams stem from . . .

Your Subconscious Desires Subconsciously, you wish to express yourself; it's as simple as that. That fertile, active, often highly creative mind of yours, teeming with ideas and impressions, must burst forth via self-expression or you are utterly miserable. Subconsciously, too, there is the wish to share, although you may not recognize it as such. There is, remember, that other Twin in you and deep in your subconscious is the desire to share all knowledge and experience with him. Of course there are numerous forms of self-expression; you can concretize your creative ideas in art, music, literature, or in smart commercial schemes. You can talk conversationally, give lectures, or even make political speeches. In one way or another, though, your subconscious desire to express yourself shows up pretty constantly in your everyday life. You are not one to sit and listen to others expounding their ideas without contributing your own views on the matter; nor are you inclined to let a criticism directed at you go unanswered. While you *can* keep a secret, others should warn you in advance if a certain matter is strictly confidential, for with your nose for news you tend to receive all bits of information as interesting bulletins to be immediately released to the general public!

In the area of personal relationships, your desire to express yourself can be a plus, as there's not likely to be a communications gap between you and another person—provided, of course, that the other person is not one of those silent, noncommunicative souls. So, you and your mate, partner, or whoever would have good rapport and exchange of mutual ideas and reactions going for you. This is assuming you always express yourself in a kindly way, which you sometimes do not. Because you are naturally high-strung and a bit tense (who wouldn't be, with air, Mercury, mutability, and Twins blended in their psyche!), you are capable of being snappish and irritable on occasion. These are passing phases, however, and you do not usually hold grudges. Hopefully, those who are the recipients of your sometimes barbed commentary will not hold grudges either.

In matters of career and finances, your subconscious wish to communicate points, as previously mentioned, to real potential in the communications fields. But in any kind of job—which could very well be clerical, for your quickness and dexterity equip you for one of those "diversified duties" office jobs—you would be happiest and most productive in an environment where you could express yourself freely. *And* where you could be on the phone a lot! You would be desolate in a job where conversation, personal phone calls, and frequent trips to the water cooler or coffee wagon were prohibited.

Dreams which leave you feeling confused, baffled, or frustrated can be your subconscious teasing and testing your powers of perception, your associative intuition to translate the symbolism into the reality. In a sense, your conscious mind and your subconscious desires may be said to represent the Gemini Twins in you, with the subconscious twin seeking to impart knowledge to the conscious twin. Fanciful, perhaps, but very appropriate. By being aware of your subconscious desires and of your unconscious instincts, you will be better able to come up with the real meanings of your dream episodes.

Your Special Abilities and Talents These are in the realm of your conscious state. In your case, your abilities and talents are so numerous it is rather difficult to pinpoint them. Actually they can be summed up in one word: versatility. There's hardly a subject that you cannot master well enough in a very short time to go out and earn a living at it, with the exception, of course, of those four-eight-and-more-year curricula in law, medicine, engineering, and so on—and even then, you'd be likely to get through more quickly than most. Your versatility is both your strength and your weakness. It's especially a weakness if you also have a very short attention span. Being versatile is to your great advantage in getting ahead in your career, in making money, in achieving special goals in life, for it enables you to utilize many possibilities in pursuing your aims. If one avenue is closed to you, you can turn your efforts to another direction—as a temporary stopgap, or as a roundabout method of getting to where you wanted to go in the first place.

Also categorized under your special abilities and talents should be your perception and intuition. You can enter a room—or meet a group of people—and perceive in a flash all the details that another person would take several hours to notice and enumerate. Nor is your perception limited to objects. You perceive people's fleeting facial expressions, subtle nuances in their voices, and revealing gestures of their hands. Nothing much escapes your perceptive powers. Added to this is your own intuition, which is a remarkable blend of previously garnered impressions and perceptions, plus an inner foresight which is right on target most of the time. Intuition is a mental faculty and is unclouded by emotions or "feelings" (psychic impressions, on the other hand, basically operate on the emotional level; but intuition is of the mind). As a Gemini, with all that emphasis on mind power, you are a natural for intuitional experience, which, indeed, you may often have, and classify it as a hunch or a lucky guess.

As you can see, you have decided assets in these various abilities and talents, but the question is: How have you made use of them? Just in case you are an ultra versatile Gemini with an ultra short attention span, you have probably not made use of them at all. In which case, your dreams are probably driving you frantic as your subconscious tries in diverse ways to get you to focus on something, anything—just focus!

With all your versatility, perception, and intuition, you really ought to be able to move mountains, once you achieve that inner direction you need. We are not suggesting that you become a totally concentrative, one-track-mind individual—nor is your subconscious suggesting this via dreams. That would be quite impossible and you would be quite miserable were you even to try for such an out-of-character about-face. Actually, you thrive on multiple interests and activities and find that a refreshing change of pace in the midst of a project is beneficial to you. For example, say you are writing an article and proceed smoothly with it for a few pages, then reach an impasse. Your impulse may be to leave the typewriter, go for a walk, phone a friend, bake a cake, or watch television. And this is very good for you, as it has the effect of plunging your mind into a different medium, which invariably produces a rush of new ideas. In brief, your natural tendency to flit about can be mentally stimulating to you, *but* the catch is to be sure you do go back and finish whatever you left in midstream. That is the secret of a successful Gemini. You can do four (or forty) things at once, but make sure you get back to them after those interruptions; otherwise you'll leave a trail that's strewn with half-finished masterpieces.

It's a safe bet that many of your dreams are giving you this same advice. You have tremendous potential, and both astrology and your dreams are aids in helping you to realize that potential. What have you done, so far, in utilizing these aids? We'd be willing to wager that if you look back and review the panorama of your life to date you'd find at least a few missed or neglected opportunities. If you'd ever finished that course in creative writing, your name might be a TV network byword today; or if you'd stayed around long enough in that job with the ad agency, you might now be its number-one account executive. Maybe in the realm of relationships, you've been a bit inconsistent too. Yes, you are exceedingly reluctant to tie yourself down to just one romance at a time, but there comes a time when quantity does not really equate with quality as found in one individual. Back there in your subconscious are kicking around lots and lots of these tentative starts, incompleted projects, unfulfilled promises; and you may wonder why your dreams sometimes leave you with a vague sort of disquietude. Your dreams reflect not only your current interests and problems, but also some of the unresolved issues of the past; they can provide keys to the solution of present problems and insight into those perplexities that are buried deep in your psyche.

How Do You Dream? You are probably one of those lucky ones who can snatch a nap anywhere. Even in short five-minute catnaps, you're likely to experience dreams that seem much longer than the five minutes. At night, in your own bed, you tend to be a restless sleeper, half awakening frequently. Your sleep period, however, is likely to be crammed full with numerous, disconnected, action-packed dream episodes, whether or not you remember them upon waking. That fertile mind of yours *never* sleeps. Have you ever seen a treadmill? That's a wheel turned by an animal treading an endless belt; the faster he runs the faster the wheel turns, but he stays in the same place. Your dreams reflect this endless mental activity. Bits and pieces of the day's events, half-remembered incidents of the recent past, hints of future probabilities, and, above all, your intuition and perception keep working at full speed whether you are awake or asleep. Along with versatility, there is a creative streak in you, and your dreams reveal this, too. You tend to dream in color, perhaps in symbols, and voices may be more audible to you in dreams than is usually the case. Needless to say, with your urge for association, scads of people come and go across the stage of your dream episodes. Your job, of course—and it's a fine mental challenge for you—is to weed out the meaningful from the day's residue in your dreams.

What Specific Dream Categories Mean to You

Confinement Dreams A ghastly thought for a Gemini! One of your basic qualities is your love of the changing scene; to be confined anywhere, even in a dream, can be traumatic. In such a dream you're in some place from which there is no exit; since in real life you instinctively look about for the exit from any place or situation in which you find yourself, in your dream episode you probably devote a good deal of attention to discovering the way out from whatever the confinement may be. Being a Gemini, your dream reaction is one of nervousness as you seek to extricate yourself from the trap (you consider any restriction a trap!). Although this sort of dream leaves you with the waking impression that you are going to be caught and confined in some way, the real meaning of this dream is that you are already caught by your own actions or words of the recent past and that you boxed yourself into that confinement situation. It may relate to a decision you made involving extra responsibility, or to your disclosure of some confidential information (which you know is going to be traced back to you). Or it may be some form of hanky-panky involving sex or cash that's got you feeling a bit uneasy these days. Anyhow, you are the one who has brought the confinement in the dream on yourself. Your subconscious is accenting your concern over the matter, which you have not fully faced up to in your waking hours.

Insecurity Dreams Join the crowd! We all have these dreams, what with the state of the world these days, and usually this type of dream features something lost, stolen, exposed, or inexplicably missing. It could be your money, car, a relative or friend, for which/whom you are frantically searching. You yourself may be lost, plunged suddenly in an unfamiliar environment with no clues as to where you are or how you got there (but you are certainly insecure about the whole thing). Very often what you dream you've lost or are searching for has nothing to do with the matter that's prompting your waking-hours insecurity. Your dream of a missing pocketbook or wallet could refer to a new job you've applied for but are not too sure you'll get, or your dream of losing some vital documents can relate to waking-hours insecurity regarding your home environment. The absence of clothing in your dream, especially when you are in a very public place, always relates to a subconscious worry about your status or reputation (are your little peccadilloes going to be exposed and result in your loss of esteem?). So if you dream you are standing stark naked in Macy's window, don't go thinking it's your irresistible sexual magnetism! It's your subconscious pointing up that sneaky little move you made recently, which could be embarrassing if it's found out. Unless you have lots of insecurity dreams, there's no need to overemphasize their importance. And when you do have one, you can easily relate it to a waking-hours feeling of insecurity, very often of very minor importance.

Frustration Dreams This is the sort of dream where you simply cannot complete what you start. Your best efforts are frustrated in some way or other. You may be trying to board a vehicle to take you some place vital, but you miss the train, bus, or whatever. Or, you're on your way to meet someone, only to find he or she isn't there. Or, the place itself, if you get to it does not at all resemble the place you were headed for. It's the failure of completion or follow-through that's the mark of a frustration dream, with, of course, the very definite personal frustration that accompanies it. One would think that a Gemini, whose failing is often that of noncompletion of projects started, would be subject to this type of dream. However, in real life, your uncompleted projects are unfinished because of your own drifting away from them, not because of any outside forces interrupting the follow-through. You seldom feel frustrated when you walk away from a brilliantly begun project, so you're not really prone to experiencing more than the average number of frustration dreams. However, your subconscious is getting a message across in such a dream. This would relate to a waking-hours condition in which you really are frustrated—another person, perhaps, who clamps the lid on your enthusiasms, or a job which you would dearly love to get out of, but haven't as yet made the right connection for a switch. The dream provides clues as to the source of your frustration, which, once identified, is more easily dealt with. An individual highlighted in your dream would have correlation with a real-life person who frustrates you (the *type* of individual, not necessarily the same person); or a dream in which you are prevented from getting to a certain place, or seeing a certain person, would represent current frustrating conditions over which you have little control at the moment.

Passive Dreams Not at all your type of dream, unless the action is awfully interesting! This is the sort of dream where you are totally detached from what's going on, watching it as a mere observer but experiencing no emotions or other reactions. In a way, you almost know you're dreaming when you have a passive dream, for the detachment is so complete that you rather feel as though you could get up and walk out any time, as at a movie, and frequently you do just that. The subject matter of the passive dream may be practically anything. It's the nonparticipation quality of it that identifies this type of dream. Your subconscious can, however, be prompting you to "get it all together" from the standpoint of organizing your life, relationships, work methods, or social interests, with a view to the overall picture. This is what the passive dream is—a glimpse of the overall scene. Accordingly, you might pick up some helpful hints in such a dream about the motives of others in your life or the logical outcome of your own recent actions. In the passive dream, you yourself may or may not be part of the action, but if you are, it is as though you were watching a mirrored reflection of yourself. That can be significant too, in terms of self-analysis or self-criticism. As with all dreams, try to remember the details for waking-hours consideration. You can train yourself to do this by literally instructing your mind, just before falling asleep, to remember the night's dreams. It might not happen the very first night you try it, but will eventually.

Action Dreams You probably have a lot of these. The action dream is noted for a good deal of physical motion: walking, running, jumping, hastening after someone or something, even doing some kind of manual labor—any action where you can almost feel the breezes rushing by as you move, or the muscles flexing in your body. This is different from the sort of dream in which you view yourself in motion; in the action dream you are not watching, you are doing. There is usually a sense of urgency. It is somehow vitally important that you get where you're going, or see that individual, or finish that piece of work. The urgency need not be at all unpleasant; as a matter of fact you feel stimulated by a sense of accomplishment in the action dream. As a Gemini, your action dream not only reflects your own innate temperament which sometimes impels you to be in a sort of perpetual-motion activity, but also in such a dream you will find that your subconscious is urging you on to a *specific* accomplishment. Going to a certain destination or setting out to see a special person could represent an opportunity (probably one which came up in the past few days) that may be job- or money-related. Your subconscious is urging you to follow through on this. A social opportunity might show up in a dream featuring your action episode in the midst of people (you may have recently had the chance to affiliate yourself with a new group whose interests could provide mental stimulation for you). The action dream fundamentally is a suggestion that you "get moving" on a specific matter.

Recurring Dreams This kind of dream is repetitious. You've had the same dream before, or one very like it, maybe more than once. If it is exactly the same dream each time, interpreting its meaning should be easier; if it is similar in theme, but different as to detail, look for the constant factor in the dream. This may be a specific individual who, if you know this person in real life, certainly has some significance to you if he or she keeps turning up in your recurring dream. Or it may be that the person in your dream represents an image or figure: an authority figure, a father or mother image, a love object, and so on. Once you identify the individual in your dream, correlate him or her to a person in your real life, and then note what he or she is doing or saying and the surroundings or action in which this individual is spotlighted. Your recurring dream may present a situation or a condition: you on your way to the airport, for example, or walking down a church aisle, or buying glamour items at a boutique, or whatever. These examples would, of course, be reasonably easy to figure out. It could mean a subconscious wish for travel, marriage, or the "good life." Analyze the people, details, and surroundings in your recurring dreams, for they can be most revealing about your deepest wishes. They can also be helpful as indicators of areas in your life which need working out or working *on*. Also under this category is the *resumed dream*, in which you wake up for some reason in the middle of the dream, then fall asleep again and resume just where you left off. This is your subconscious refusing to be diverted from the message it is trying to get across to you, so make a note of those waking memories and the impressions left by such a dream—they are important.

Escape Dreams You love these and probably wish you could have them more often. In such a dream you are making your escape from what's bothering you in real life. What could be nicer! There's a feeling of happy finality in the escape dream as you takeoff into the wild blue yonder (literally or figuratively) or you make your exit from someplace and close the door behind you. Or perhaps you find yourself in a totally new environment without a care in the world. All these lovely, impossible dreams are most enjoyable and certainly stem from the subconscious desire to escape responsibility, work, restrictions, and frustrations. Once in a while there will be a real clue in such a dream, for your subconscious can point up a way to ease your burdens a bit. This could take the form of an individual featured in the dream, who can be translated into a real-life person; or if any matter of choice is shown in the escape dream, however minor, this can be a clue to possible alternative action that you should consider. Mostly, though, the typical escape dream performs its function by lessening the tensions and releasing the pressures of everyday life. Your subconscious is fulfilling your desire, if only in a dream.

Sex Dreams Whether or not your sex dreams involve a partner (and with a Gemini, they usually do), the basic thrust of such a dream relates to the quality of your sex life in waking hours. Invariably, frequent sex dreams mean that the individual is not satisfied with his or her sex life and the subconscious seeks to compensate for this in dreams. However, as a Gemini, you have a further complication concerning your innate hesitance to make a total commitment in many areas, including relationships. As a result, your sex life may be active, varied, and experimental, but the quantity may not make up for the lack of quality. This, of course, also is dependent on your personal standards of behavior. Although a sexual encounter does not necessarily spell total commitment, you have a subconscious sense of responsibility about sex, although your verbalized attitude toward it in real life may belie that fact. Accordingly, your sex dreams can have deeper meanings than mere physical pleasure, or dream compensation for lack of sexual satisfaction in your waking hours. In your sex dreams, your partner somehow represents your ideal of a mate—an ideal for whom you may be searching in real life, or may have found but walked away from. Your sex dreams tend either to leave bittersweet memories upon awakening or to be nonorgasmic, leaving you somewhat frustrated. All of which ties in with your ambivalent attitude toward sex (the Twins, again!) in which half of you wants to be free, while the other half wants to find the ideal union. Your subconscious may help you to work this out via your sex dreams.

Sensuous Dreams These are usually nonsexual, but feature one or more of the senses—sight, hearing, smell, taste, and touch. Voices are not infrequent in your dreams. You may even have experienced the hearing of voices in that twilight period just prior to dropping off to sleep. These are all messages for

Gemini the communicator! Your sensuous dreams may include eating food, seeing sharply defined objects (more clearly than in the usual vague, misty dream visions), smelling perfume, or touching an object that feels just exactly as it would when you touch it in real life. However, the sounds you hear are likely to be most important in your sensuous dreams. It may be merely a voice calling your name over and over—that's a real attention getter, and it is your subconscious hauling you back from whatever tempting byway you're currently exploring in waking hours, because there's something important you should focus on. Or it may be conversation you hear or in which you participate—and usually there will be some key phrase that sticks with you upon awakening. It may not seem to make sense, but it does, so analyze it. You may hear city sounds or country sounds, music or dissonance, but somewhere in that welter of sound your subconscious is giving you a message that relates to a current situation in your life, along with a suggestion of how to handle it. Other kinds of sensuous dreams relate, if pleasant, to some sort of sense satisfaction you crave (dreaming of eating rich food, if you're on a diet, for example). If the dreams are unpleasant, your subconscious is telling you to tone down some form of overindulgence.

Precognitive Dreams You might have a precognitive dream once in a while, but as your intuition is usually operative during your waking hours, your glimpses of the future are not limited to dreams. In the precognitive dream, what you dream about comes true in the immediate future, exactly as dreamed or close enough to be identifiable. The dream may be of any subject, and the importance of the event itself either major or minor. It will make enough of an impact, though, to show you that you are tuned into the cosmic stream. Sometimes, if you have not trained yourself to remember and record dream episodes, you may awaken from a precognitive dream with an impression of impending disaster or excitement. Think how nice it would be if you could remember the details of the dream that led to that impression, as you would then be forearmed for the disaster or primed for the excitement. Incidentally, "impending disaster" often manifests itself in merely a small disappointment, so don't get carried away. You are not as likely to experience precognitive dreams as are some people, however, for your intuitive faculties are already functioning at a high level.

Peopled Dreams Many people come and go, quite casually, in your dreams. If you're a typical Gemini you know loads of people in your real life, and though you may not be all that close to most of them, your list of acquaintances is probably quite lengthy. So it is not out of character for you to have peopled dreams. It will be when an individual or a group in your dream is speaking or behaving totally unlike their real-life counterparts that you should carefully note the difference. This sort of dream could be your subconscious revealing to you a person's real motives, as opposed to his or her surface personality. Someone you dislike could show up in your dream as a real good guy or gal, revealing the real character of the person, which you, in your skim-the-surface Gemini way, have not noticed (despite your perceptive powers). Or the reverse may be true. In any case, among all the people in your dreams, some will stand out for one reason or another and these are the ones to note and analyze.

Symbols in Dreams Dreams are literally fraught with symbolism, but occasionally you will have a dream in which a specific object, color, number, design, pattern, or animal emerges in such a meaningful way that it's simply got to be a symbol for something significant. Astrology is also fraught with symbolism, principal among which are the elements into which the signs are divided: fire, earth, air, and water—symbolizing the spirit, the body, the mind, and the emotions, respectively. The element of air is especially applicable to you, an air sign. A dream of flying, for example, or a dream in which you are particularly conscious of the air you breathe, or of breezes playing on you or wind rushing about you, is a reminder from your subconscious that your natural environment is the world of the mind and that you have the perception, logic, and analytical powers to resolve just about any problem. Fire-related dreams are also compatible with your temperament and signify spiritual awareness. As to other symbols in your dreams, what they mean to *you* and the impression they leave with you are your clues for correlation with waking-hours events. If you should dream of the number seven, or the color yellow, or a pair of anything (doors, keys, kittens, paths, cups, or even a set of salt and pepper shakers), that dream will have extra meaning. It is your subconscious dramatizing your own symbolism and possibly revealing the key to an identity problem, or even the overall direction your life should be following.

Chapter 7

Cancer

(June 22–July 23)

Your unconscious produces your basic, natural instincts, while your subconscious reveals your deepest desires and wishes. Your Sun sign sets the stamp of your own individuality on both your unconscious instincts and your subconscious desires—all of which are reflected in your dreams.

CANCER is a water sign, ruled by the Moon, cardinal in quality (which means action-oriented). The watery element and the changeability of the Moon (which never shows exactly the same face one night after the other) combine to make you emotional, sensitive, impressionable, and *changeable.* Although the cardinality of your sign does indicate your ambition and impulse to be constantly moving ahead toward the desired goal, yours is not the head-on, headstrong, direct way. You're far too sensitive to risk falling flat on your face in full view of spectators as you pursue special goals. You operate in a roundabout, indirect sort of maneuvering manner, which can often bring remarkable results. It's just that it is not always obvious to others that you're going where you're going until suddenly they see you there—in the top spot! Cancer children are often shy, with a strong bond to the mother; Cancer adults learn to build up a facade of confidence over their shyness, but usually retain close ties to the family. You could have a specific creative talent, and despite all that shyness and emotional sensitivity, you can be outstandingly hardheaded and practical in money matters. You're well equipped for a career in the arts or in finance, in counseling, medicine, or anything connected with liquids (milk, soft drinks, liquor, even oil!). Your own emotional orientation makes you sympathetic and understanding of others and their problems.

Your Unconscious Instincts You have strong urges to "preserve and protect"—and if that sounds like a quote from the Constitution of the United States, it is—and not surprising, either, as the United States also has a Cancer Sun sign. Your urge to preserve can show up in small ways, such as your compulsion never to throw anything away, or in your attraction to antiques (perhaps as a collector), or in the way in which you keep in touch with old friends and remember anniversaries and birthdays and so on. It could also be in your maintenance of the family as a unit, or your frequent visits to the old family home. You remember; and remembering is one way of preserving. You may be conservative in the sense that you prefer to keep well-worn but carefully preserved old furnishings rather than make a clean sweep and redecorate your home with the latest trendy items. You have a real affection for what is familiar and comforting. In personal relationships, your urge to preserve can be expressed in a positive way through loyalty to long-time friends, really working at a marriage to preserve it, or staying with the firm you start out with and working your way to the top. You like continuity in your life.

In a negative way, your urge to preserve can be manifested in your tendency never to forget a problem or an injury, and to rehash it over and over again ad infinitum. Or in a relationship you could be ultra clinging, super possessive, the motive being preserving the status quo of the alliance, though this sometimes has just the opposite effect!

Your urge to protect is evident in your "mothering" instinct. Whether you are a male or a female, there is a definite maternal streak in you, which is why you listen to and sympathize with friends' problems, feed them wonderfully, and make them as cozy and comfortable as possible; it's your instinct to protect your loved ones. All of which is a great comfort to those lucky enough to be included on your list of loved ones. Of course this, too, like all good things, can be overdone a bit, but your motive to protect is admirable.

On a larger stage, it may be your career, your community, or your country toward which you direct your instincts to preserve and protect. (There are a lot of Cancerians in politics.) And if you are a positive, highly evolved Cancerian, these instincts can lead you toward humanitarian expression in which you can work wonders for those in need. You have a special sympathy for little children and for elderly people, and Cancerians in medicine tend toward pediatrics and geriatrics.

These unconscious urges to preserve and protect are innate in you, part of your totality, and hence show up occasionally in dreams. However, the major portion of your dreams are generated by . . .

Your Subconscious Desires Chief among these is your desire for security. The security wished for may be material, emotional, or spiritual, but is very much a part of almost all that motivates you. Stemming from this desire for security is your much-written-about domesticity. It is not true that all Cancerians love to cook, to do housework, or to spend their afternoons making slipcovers! You may or may not like all those little nitty-gritty homemaking details, but what you do want and need and wish for, subconsciously, is to have established roots.

The home is a visible symbol of roots, and therefore the connection between Cancerians and domesticity. You may be quite a traveler, spending your days flitting hither, thither, and yon; nevertheless, you want a haven to which you can retreat when the world gets to be too much. That haven represents your security. The haven itself is not only a material symbol of security, but you derive emotional and spiritual sustenance from it as well. A Cancerian without a place to call home is in a sad plight, indeed, for he or she would tend to feel very insecure and disoriented. Also, because you have a smart business head on your shoulders, you prefer to own your home rather than pay rent to a landlord.

Having gotten you securely established in that haven you so greatly desire, we turn to the question of your emotional security. As a water-sign person, you are emotion-oriented, which means that in a showdown your heart would probably rule your head. It also means that despite flexible contemporary moral standards, you as a Cancerian find more emotional fulfillment within a framework of security and permanence. You're the marrying type, you really are! While marriage is no guarantee of either security or permanence, there are certain advantages, especially if you are a Cancerian female, for you do tend to think of not only the emotional security but of the financial ramifications inherent in that marriage license. Also there is the question of children; with the strong maternal streak of Cancer, you could very well hope to bear or adopt a child, and with that combined preserve/protect/ security impetus of yours, you'd want a stable background for the youngster.

In your job/career/financial aims, security is a high priority, too. You'd be inclined to opt for the job with the best fringe benefits and retirement program over the kind of job where your income could fluctuate widely. The best sort of commission arrangement might appeal to you less than a more moderate but guaranteed salary. However, you do have a flair for moneymaking and, once assured of your steady income, might do quite well in speculative sidelines, such as real estate.

Probably your most unpleasant dreams are ones expressing insecurity, which you might find popping up mostly when there is some waking-hours security factor to which you have not faced up. It might be an emotional relationship that you subconsciously fear is deteriorating, or a property matter that has developed disquieting symptoms, but which you don't want to admit to yourself. Your subconscious is invariably working on your side. It could be producing in your dreams the events or problems that are most important to you, providing clues as to solutions. Your dreams can also pinpoint certain traits which it might be helpful for you to develop or tone down—maybe specific talents you have but which you are not consciously aware of possessing. By understanding your subconscious desires and how these motivate and color your views, and by understanding your unconscious instincts as well, you will be better equipped to translate your dream episodes, correlating them to life situations.

Your Special Abilities and Talents These are in the area of your consciousness, as opposed to your subconscious and unconscious states. Your best abilities and talents undoubtedly include your flair for handling money matters, for doing good things with land or property, such as restoring old houses (for both the esthetic and financial benefits you derive from it), or for being the best host or hostess of the Zodiac (no small accomplishment, for aside from the pleasure your hospitality gives family and friends, many a super business deal is made in just the sort of social setting you can provide). You also have that talent for counseling—for dealing with people on a one-to-one basis, particularly where emotional or personality problems are involved. Referring again to the domestic theme, you have a decided talent for creating a home away from home, and your loved ones will never languish in a barren hotel room on a trip if you are around to provide those homey, familiar touches of comfort.

Your abilities also include a very subtle executive talent. You do not especially care to be the one who gives the orders, or even the one who receives the praise for a mission accomplished; but you do have a definite ability to be an opinion maker, to influence those who do give the orders from your behind-the-scenes position. At heart, you're a "power behind the throne" and derive great satisfaction from seeing your ideas carried out, your plans put into operation.

Of course you may not have fully utilized your talents and abilities as yet. Some carried-over shyness from your childhood may have prevented you from stepping out on your own, in full command of your potential. Or perhaps you've allowed your very real need for encouragement from those you love to snowball out of proportion. There's a bit of the baby in every Cancerian, and the tendency to wait for that coaxing, cajoling, petting, and persuading that was lavished on one in childhood, before stepping out bravely into the big world. You're lucky if you have someone who will provide this sort of encouragement, but if you don't, you should not permit this to deter you from making the most of opportunities and of your own latent talents and abilities. Your dreams could be telling you the same thing, in your nightly excursions into sleep.

With your occasional infatuation with the past, do a bit of inventorying of your life to date and of how you used, misused, or failed to use some of your fine abilities and talents. You'll probably dredge up at least a few incidents that related to your own moodiness. The Moon's rulership of your sign makes you changeable and that surely reflects in your shifts of mood. How about the time when your introverted mood prevented you from making a dynamic impression on a prospective boss and you were passed over for a more outgoing type? Or when you allowed personal sensitivity to someone's unthinking remark to plunge you into the doldrums for days and you missed out on an exciting party? Or that special relationship, where some minor incident caused you to sulk for weeks, and instead of coming around to coax you into reconciliation, the guy or gal blithely pranced off with another love partner?

Your dreams may include a lot of over-and-done-with material, for you do have that inclination to revive, even relive, prior problems. Usually, though, there will also be a link to a current situation when you dream of people or incidents long gone—hence your subconscious alerts you to the fact that if a certain line of action didn't work before, it probably won't work now, either.

Both astrology and dreams are forms of guidance and can point the way to a fuller life, a fuller realization of your potential. For example, if you experience a number of insecurity, frustration, or confinement dreams, it's a safe bet that your waking hours do not provide even your minimum material or emotional security needs or offer opportunities to express your strong urges to nourish, protect, and preserve in either a personal or career context. But your dreams are also providing clues on how to improve the situation. If they are not actual clues or clear-cut pictures of the actual situation (including some of those little facets you've failed or refused to see), they serve as a stimulus for you yourself to take the needed action for improvement.

How Do You Dream? Snuggled up nice and cozy, no doubt, but that is not exactly what is meant by the question. It's the quality and subject matter of your dreams that are significant. For one thing, you undoubtedly experience a lot of emotional reactions in your dreams and are unlikely to have many dreams in which you are the detached, objective, nonfeeling observer. Your natural instinct is to involve yourself emotionally in real life, to identify with others and their problems and their joys. As a matter of fact, your being a water-sign person makes it difficult for you to depersonalize anyway, asleep or awake. Therefore, you are probably the one who awakens with tears on your cheeks or a smile on your lips. Participation in complicated emotional issues in dreams can be a bit of a drain and you may wake up sometimes slightly exhausted from the turmoil of it all. Your subconscious could be *trying* to tell you not to get so involved in real-life emotional situations, especially if you really should be a mere onlooker instead of plunging into the center of a volatile situation. Could it be: your sister-in-law's problem with *her* sister? A co-worker's feud with a neighbor? Your cousin's temporary rift with his or her mate? Even when your dreams are not pleasant, though, you don't like to wake up, as sleep is an escape for you, most comforting and exhilarating when you have enjoyable dreams.

What Specific Dream Categories Mean to You

Confinement Dreams This is when you dream you cannot get out of whatever unnamed spot you find yourself in during the dream. There's usually an accompanying feeling of apprehension, too, for you would not be confined unless something bad were going to happen to you. If as a child you were closed up in a room for punishment, this could have left its mark on your psyche, intensifying your fear in the dream. It does not change the basic meaning of such a dream, however, for the confinement dream represents imprisonment of your own making. Just as your childhood confinement may have been a punishment for being naughty, your adult confinement dream is also a "punishment" for having done something that makes you feel guilty. It may have been a recent but minor incident. Nevertheless, your little guilt feeling got buried in your subconscious, which obliges you by administering the punishment you basically feel you deserve. The scene or details of the dream do not matter so much; it is the feeling of confinement that's important. But when you realize that you have indeed confined yourself, and when you have pinpointed what you've done (major or minor) that makes you feel the need for confinement (i.e. punishment), then you are not likely to experience that dream again. This type of dream can be therapeutic in terms of bringing that festering "guilt" from your subconscious into the clear light of day (your conscious state).

Insecurity Dreams These are by far the most prevalent kind of dream, as almost everyone feels insecure about something. Given your Cancerian need for security, these dreams may be quite distressing—not necessarily to the point of panic, but enough so that you awaken with a rather gloomy outlook for the day. Usually these dreams involve the loss of—or the search for—something that represents security to you. Most common of lost dream objects is the purse or wallet. This may or may not represent a waking-hours insecurity involving money—that depends on whether or not money is a symbol of security to you. The lost wallet can also relate to emotional insecurity. For you, a Cancerian, insecurity dream symbols are interchangeable. Dreaming of a lost or missing person (child, family member, friend) might represent a waking-hours insecurity regarding finances. You can probably identify the area of real insecurity by assessing your emotional reaction in the dream. If you're weeping out of all proportion over the loss of a purse with five dollars in it, the dream undoubtedly relates to a deeper insecurity, such as in your love life. Insecurity dreams can also present you wearing very little clothing in a situation where you should be dressed to the hilt—or wearing an old dress or suit to an elegant gala! This sort of dream means you're insecure about your status or reputation for some reason. You do not want others to see you partially or poorly clad, but in your dream they do. This may refer to some little question of pride on your part, or to your fear of exposure. Maybe you initiated a bit of inaccurate gossip and you're afraid it will be traced back to you. Or perhaps it could be a mild flirtation with your best friend's mate, which got a bit out of hand.

Frustration Dreams The hallmark of a frustration dream is that you cannot complete something you start or something you desire desperately to accomplish. Maybe you awaken before you've had the chance to do whatever it was you planned, or the dream suddenly switches around in that disconcerting way dreams have, and you're someplace else, with that gnawing sense of frustration crowding in on you. In your Cancerian way you will, of course, brood over this throughout the dream, and maybe even brood about it during the next day's waking hours. Actually, this type of dream is not as hard on you as it is on some. You do not enjoy being frustrated, but it doesn't usually drive you up the wall the way it does some people (Ariens, for instance). However, this type of dream can be revealing if it pinpoints the source of one of your waking-hours frustrations: a certain individual, an insurmountable problem, maybe one of your own negative traits that you're trying to overcome, or a talent that you are desperately striving to develop. Don't forget that the characters in your dreams are sometimes extensions of yourself. If you have a frustration dream featuring a person who frustrates you via one of your own traits, it's your subconscious reminding you to persevere. Once you identify the source of your frustration in the dream, and subsequently correlate it to the real-life source, your conscious mind will be able to take over and cope with it. At this point your frustration dreams will fade away.

Passive Dreams You don't have to do anything at all in the passive dream; just lie there and watch. Being a Cancerian, you are not naturally inclined to play the role of objective observer. Since you are basically emotionally oriented, you do tend to get involved in issues, plots, and personalities, even in your dreams. However, in the passive dream—which could be described as a dream which unfolds on a screen, with you as the audience of one—your subconscious is giving you a hint that it is a good thing sometimes to step away from the heat of the fray (the emotional involvement) and view matters objectively. In this sort of dream, you yourself may be among the performers in the play—a play is really what the passive dream resembles—and your subconscious may provide you with insight into the plot that might not be possible if you were not on the sidelines observing your own image. This sort of dream usually leaves you feeling more thoughtful than anything else—and probably a good thing, too, as it enables you to assess the dream action without personal bias.

Action Dreams A healthy sort of dream for you to have, as it concretizes into physical activity certain of your subconscious desires or incipient plans. In this sort of dream you are moving about physically—not in the usual vague, somewhat disembodied manner so common in dreams, but in such a way that you actually feel the ground under your feet. The objects you touch are sharply defined and real, and you are aware of your muscles working as you run, walk, shake hands, or hammer a nail. This is a healthy sort of dream for you because it enables you, in the dream, to act out some suppressed wish or desire. That run down the street, featured in your dream, expresses your eagerness to achieve a career goal or a financial objective. You are on the run after it, and this can set the stage for a real action day in that area during your waking hours. Or you may dream of running upstairs, which could symbolize aspiration in action. Or it could be a dream of hurrying after an individual. That could be you in pursuit of a certain relationship, being less reserved than usual. The basic meaning of the action dream is that your subconscious is telling you the time is ripe for waking-hours action on the matter that correlates with your dream.

Recurring Dreams This is the same dream you keep experiencing, maybe over a period of years, once in a while or fairly frequently. Needless to say, there's something important here that your subconscious is trying to get across to you—or, having gotten it across once, there is some need for a further reminder now and then. Whatever the theme of this recurring dream—and whether or not it is an exact repeat in every detail—look for the constant factor in the dream each time it occurs. Does it leave you with an impression of joy, fear, frustration, insecurity, hope, or the nagging sense that you've forgotten something vital? The clue to the recurring dream is the impression it makes on *you* and how it relates to a situation or event in your current life. It may be that you tend to get into similar real-life situations over and over again, without learning from past experience (like falling in love with a certain type of individual whom you know is not good for you). So each time you get into such a situation, the recurring dream pops up. Once again it is your subconscious trying to drive a point home to you!

Escape Dreams These are pleasant dreams and there should be more of them! In the escape dream you leave behind you all your worries and cares by escaping into a new environment, out of a place of confinement and into freedom. Freedom and a happy-go-lucky feeling are the keynotes of the escape dream, which of course reflect your subconscious desire to free yourself of certain responsibilities or burdens. In these dreams your subconscious is providing you with simple pleasures, and incidentally providing a release from built-up tensions and pressures. It might be said that you experience the escape dream when you need it most. Aside from its therapeutic value (it does leave you with a more positive outlook for the following day), it is the easiest to interpret. You want out—and in your dream this wish is satisfied.

Sex Dreams Your sex dreams probably include a lot of foreplay, and this ties in with one of your deepest desires—to be babied and petted. Translated into adult sexual experience, this desire would attract you as much to the prelude to sex as to the sex act itself. Although your waking hours may include sufficient sexual activity for your needs, if they do not also include heaps of affection you are likely to have this subconscious need satisfied via frequent sex dreams. Also, to you, whether you realize it or not, sex is not only a physical drive, but a source of comfort, reassurance, and a sort of reward. If things aren't going all that well in your life, sexual pleasure can make you feel that at least "somebody cares." This is in line, too, with your occasional self-pitying moods and again relates to your desire to be babied and comforted; solitary sex in your dreams reveals more of the same. Frequently in dreams one finds that he or she is having sex with the most unlikely person imaginable! This can mean an unrecognized or unacknowledged sexual attraction to the person in your dream, but it is even more likely that the sex partner in your dreams is the image or figure of what you desire in a partner. (To dream you are having sex with your elderly family doctor may mean you subconsciously are attracted to older men; or to dream of a sex episode with a friend's young daughter could mean you're subconsciously attracted to teen-age girls.) It's true that one's "repressed desires" do tend to show up in dreams, possibly even more so in the area of sex; but this does give you a fuller understanding of your own complexities, which are easier to deal with via the conscious mind when recognized.

Sensuous Dreams You are naturally a sensuous person, over and above sex-related sensuousness. This type of dream rarely features sex, but emphasizes the senses of sight, hearing, smell, taste, and touch. You may taste or touch in other dreams, but without experiencing the reality of those senses. In the sensuous dream you actually savor the food, or the wine, or whatever, and you can *feel* the object your fingers touch. Sense satisfaction is particularly important to you (being a gourmet cook would appeal to you, and you revel in the feel of soft fabrics, plushy upholstery). This desire for sense satisfaction is revealed in your dreams, particularly in the sensuous dream, where it is the most realistic and fulfilling. Your sensuous dreams, when pleasing and enjoyable, actually represent a small satisfaction in recent waking hours. The real-life incident may not correlate to the dream episode, but the feeling of satisfaction is there. It could be a job promotion, for example, for which you worked hard, or a party you gave, which went off exactly as planned. If your sensuous dream finds you feeling slightly bilious after stuffing yourself with rich goodies, or skinning your fingers on an abrasive surface, your subconscious is reminding you that you are not indestructible and should perhaps tone down a tendency to overindulge.

Precognitive Dreams In these dreams, which may be about any subject under the sun, your awareness that you've had a precognitive dream only comes a few days later when the dream is mirrored in reality. Sometimes the reality is an exact repeat of the dream itself; more often it has to do with the quality of the dream rather than its content. For example, you may dream that you're going to meet someone who doesn't show up and in the dream you experience a sharp sense of disappointment; a few days later you hear from the college of your son's choice that he has not been accepted for admittance. That is a dream disappointment followed by a real-life disappointment though the subject matter differed. In your dream you might suddenly find some money, which surprises and pleases you; shortly thereafter, a former romantic interest may reenter your life, surprising and pleasing you. (Unless you tend to have precognitive dreams which are exact repeats, don't expect actually to find money!) As a water-sign individual, you tend to be somewhat psychic, psychic ability being related to the emotions and feelings, which are more powerful in water signs. Accordingly—and depending on your attitude toward, and receptivity to, psychic phenomena—you may experience dreams in which your psychic ability manifests itself. In such a dream, you *know* that it is not a "regular" dream, but a psychic experience. Bridging the usual levels of the unconscious, subconscious, and conscious states, the psychic forces are revealed in your dream and you are at all times during the dream aware of them. The dream itself may, again, concern any subject or person, and represents an advance view of an incident that is soon to occur. A truly psychic dream can, naturally, be of much help in preparing you for either the pleasure or the problem foretold.

Peopled Dreams As a Cancerian, you are concerned with people—sensitive to their needs, sympathetic to their problems, and so on. And because you have this impulse to identify with others, to personalize even somewhat impersonal types of relationships, you tend to dream of specific people as opposed to the faceless crowds that show up in the dreams of individuals born under some of the other signs. You can spend a whole night's dream episodes involved with merely one or two persons, and even when your dreams are of seemingly unconnected segments, the same individuals may pop up in all of the segments. This reflects your waking-hours preoccupation with the personalities and interests of those around you. If you can identify the specific individuals in your dreams (who are not always the individuals they appear to be), your peopled dreams can provide you with hints on how to handle situations involving these persons. For instance, although your night may be filled with dreams about your boss, or your sister-in-law's nephew, who is trying to tell you something important—that person may actually represent a friend who wishes to confide a personal problem to you, but hasn't quite summoned up the courage to do so. Look for similarities of personality, mannerisms, or reactions between the dream figure and a real person you know. In this particular example, the dream figure may manifest nervousness or embarrassment in his attempts to tell you something, which could clue you in to the real person's current state of mind regarding the confidence. This, of course, is merely an example, but frequently you have to do a lot of detective work in interpreting dreams!

Symbols in Dreams While there is much symbolism in dreams, once in a while you will have a dream in which some special symbol is highlighted. Often this is an object such as a single rose, a shoe, an animal, an abstract design, a candle, a number, or a color. Don't go tying everything in with phallic symbolism, for as often as not the symbol will have a quite different meaning. Dreaming of a symbol is important strictly in terms of what the symbol means to *you.* If you adore birds, rubies, exotic wine bottles, mountains, and the color magenta, dreaming of one of these is symbolically positive and can represent a recent or soon-to-be-realized pleasure. On the other hand, if you dislike turtles, airplanes, geraniums, jade, and the number four, dreaming of one of these represents an unpleasant condition you are currently coping with or a slight apprehension of some future event. In astrology, the symbolism of the elements is important: fire equates with spirit, earth with the material body, air with the mind, water with the emotions. Water is particularly meaningful to you since Cancer is a water sign. If you dream of a body of water, of swimming, boating, rain, or some other watery subject, assess the dream carefully for it can be very revealing as to your emotional state or the progress of a relationship, and perhaps provide some insight into how you express your emotions. If you should dream of the number two, the color silver gray, or a shellfish (all very Cancerian), your subconscious could be prompting you, through symbolism, to unearth latent talents, confirm your basic identity, even perhaps supplying you with a vital key to your true life goal.

Chapter 8

Leo

(July 24–August 23)

Your natural instincts emerge from your unconscious, while your deepest desires (sometimes unrecognized or unacknowledged) are found in your subconscious. Your Sun sign is the essential you, in terms of your own individualistic, unique qualities and traits—through which your unconscious instincts and subconscious desires operate. Because you are a Leo, the contents and meanings of your dreams reflect your own individuality, as differentiated from those of other signs.

LEO is a fire sign, ruled by the Sun, fixed in quality (which means stable, secure). The blend of fire and fixity in your Sun sign *can* make you invincible, for the fiery enthusiasm, aspiration, and idealism—when linked to the "fixed" qualities of determination, certitude, and perseverance—is a combination that can take you far. Of course we are not guaranteeing that just because you're a Leo you will automatically reach the pinnacle of success, but you do have a head start in that direction. You are at your best in a life style which includes a certain amount of authority and a great deal of on-view activity. Your executive and leadership talents stem largely from your own self-confidence and the urge to direct others. Because you are rarely indecisive, your own belief in your convictions generates in others the confidence to follow where you lead. And because of your ingrained conviction that center stage is your natural habitat, in no way are you about to do your leading from some little out-of-the-way corner! Whatever your field of dynamic activity (entertainment, finance, education, and various forms of creative expression are highlighted for Leos), your urge is to both innovate and build. You do not (like fire-sign Aries) begin a venture, then quickly go on to a new challenge, nor do you (like fixed-sign Taurus) contentedly take years and years to build the superstructure on your sound foundation. Your way is to initiate a project, liberally stamping it with your own flair for originality, and then to build on it—practically, sensibly, but at a good, quick pace.

Your Unconscious Instincts You have strong urges to rule and to create. Many of your aims and actions flow from these unconscious instincts. Your urge to rule is behind your impetus to achieve social popularity—to "dominate the scene." You do this in diverse ways: through charm, friendliness, your vivacious personality, and articulate manner of self-expression. You also see to it that others have a good time, but you see to it from the position of "*numero uno*"! It's as natural to you as breathing to propel yourself into not only the midst of the action, but into the spotlighted area of the action. In your domestic life you also tend to "rule the roost," and in one way or another, family plans are dependent on your wishes, schedule, or strategy. Only if you are a negative Leo will you do this in a "bossy" manner. Usually, others are only too happy to concur with your wishes. Like the Sun that is the symbol of your sign, you generate a lot of warmth. Yours is a very strong personality—one's personality being the outward expression of very basic, unconscious urges—which often results in your actually creating the moods of others. When you are happy, everyone around you is happy, relaxed, optimistic. When you are unhappy (or angry) others become uneasy or, figuratively, shiver in their boots. In other words, you dominate the scene with your own moods, emotions, and reactions, which is not at all true of everyone. Some people can be elated, furious, on cloud nine, or down in the dumps, without leaving the least bit of an impression on those around them—but not Leo! Of course with this unique kind of personality force goes a responsibility. Since you do affect the lives of those around you so definitively, it behooves you to use this power in a positive way, for your good and for theirs.

Your urge to create is also symbolically linked with the Sun, ruler of your sign. The Sun is the life giver inasmuch as it is the Sun's magnetic force that holds the solar system together. Physical, mental, artistic creativity are fulfilling to you, because creativity is one of your natural functions. For example, if you are a parent (having created a child) you do not take this responsibility lightly. Your child will have all that it is possible for you to give, not only in a material way but also in terms of training and education. You will instill ideals and standards of integrity in the youngster. If you have artistic or interpretive talent, you tend to work hard to develop it, utilize it, and present it for the world to see. You are competitive in what could be called an affirmative sort of way. You *assume* that you will do better than others rather than specifically compete with them to do so. You are a creative thinker in business and finance (with a special flair for speculation), an "idea person" whose ideas bear the stamp of your own personalized creativity.

Your unconscious instincts are always at work, whether you are asleep or awake, acting as the backstage props of your dreams. However, for the most part your dreams flow from . . .

Your Subconscious Desires Subconsciously you desire to love and to be loved. You will probably say that these desires are very much a part of your conscious, waking life, too, which is indeed true in reference to specific personal relationships. But your subconscious desires to love and to be loved show up in your dreams in various ways, and in your waking life are the basis for many of your actions and reactions that are seemingly unrelated to love. An example might be found in one of your favorite waking fantasies—the one where you have done some special deed or accomplished an outstanding feat. In this fantasy, you are praised, respected, admired, fussed over, and generally given the V.I.P. treatment by one and all. In fact everyone *loves* you! For your part, you are more than generous in sharing the fruits of your accomplishment, in magnanimously forgiving those who hurt or doubted you, in bestowing gifts, money (or whatever other goodies your fantasy has provided you) on all and sundry. A veritable love affair between you and the multitudes! Actually you are a generous, magnanimous person, who forgives those who hurt you. Only if the culprit happens to be right there when you first realize the hurt, will he or she bear the full brunt of your anger, which can be quite awe-inspiring. However, if the transgressor escapes your initial wrath, he or she can feel relatively safe, for you find it almost impossible to "stay mad." The fact is, you are naturally inclined to possess a wide spectrum of nice, healthy, admirable, and upbeat traits that really *are* very lovable; and you are also naturally inclined to love your fellow humans, to spread your love around among many—which may not always go over too well with your one-and-only until he or she recognizes the fact that your "regal" calling necessitates a wide range of reciprocal love, though not necessarily of an intimate, personal nature. Your sign symbol, the Lion, is after all the

King of the Beasts and in every Leo there's at least a touch of the royal attitude.

Although you are ambitious and can be a good moneymaker or a fine administrator in spiritual, material, humanitarian, or creative fields, a good part of your motivation for achievement includes the desire to please, astound, or otherwise impress others—and the really basic, unconscious motivation is to make them love you. Unless you are a most negatively polarized Leo—in which case your self-involvement is so intense and your ego so large that there is no room for anyone else in your life—love (and specifically the interflow of love) is truly your guiding influence. This is additionally symbolized by the heart which is the part of the body ruled by Leo.

In your dreams, whether they are clear-cut and readily identifiable or vague and veiled, your subconscious desires are coming to light. They are not always in a form that you recognize at first when you awake, but they are nevertheless the basis for much that occurs in your nightly dream state. In your waking hours you are a direct nondevious type of individual, and if you had your choice you would always dream of tangible matters, clearly defined. However, your subconscious does not always operate in that manner, and in many an oblique way presents for your consideration the sort of dream in which there are elements of the unknown (where are you? where are you going? who are those people? and so on). This sort of dream would tend to disturb you more than it would, say, a Piscean or a Sagittarian, for you are a positive personality and tend to make definite plans and to have explicit opinions. The purpose of one of these vague, indefinite dreams could well be to remind you that flexibility is often desirable under certain circumstances. By analyzing the dream, identifying the symbolism, and so on, the area in which your subconscious is pointing up the need for flexibility can be determined. You will also frequently find that a specific relationship shows up somewhere in the dream and that your unconscious instinct to dominate another, as well as your subconscious desire to be loved (admired, respected, recognized), will play their roles in the dream episode. Flexibility in the give-and-take of various relationships might, for example, be the message of one of these apparently vague dreams.

Your Special Abilities and Talents These should be fairly obvious, since they occupy the realm of your conscious state, your waking-hours awareness. You are undoubtedly aware of many of your strong points, such as your ability to hold to a conviction, ideal, or purpose even in the face of opposition or challenge, as well as your ability to complete what you begin through concentration and sustained effort. You have an ability to make personal sacrifices for someone you love. Though Leo is not innately a sign of sacrifice, when motivated by love you are able to submerge your own desires for the good of another. You are also able to make decisions and stick to them. A natural leader, you accept the responsibility for your actions.

With regard to your talents, many a clue is found in your sign ruler, the Sun, focal point of our solar system. Administrative areas of business and finance are highlighted, for money (as well as the Sun's magnetic force) "makes the world go 'round." There is also an accent on the more speculative side of financial operations—a job or career in the investment field, banking, insurance, or with a loan company could be your type of work. The entire entertainment field is also a "natural" for Leos. Whether you are a performer, manager, producer, director, creator, or interpreter, there's a distinctly show-biz flair in your makeup. Somewhere between the fields of investment and entertainment is the field of sports, which is both entertaining and speculative, and is another Leo type of activity. You could be an athlete, or the promoter of a sports figure; manager of a ball club or its star pitcher or quarterback. You may also merely enjoy an occasional day at the track, but the interest in sports is there.

Your talents might, however, lie in another direction and this relates to education, children, and young people. Leos are splendid educators, for as teachers they have that certain spark which ignites students' interest and aspiration; as administrators, they are capable of the overview in academic matters, and are not inclined to get bogged down in petty, personality-oriented clashes with staff. As a Leo, you also have great affinity with the young, whatever your age, and can express the right blend of understanding and authority, sympathy and objectivity. Given your own special brand of magnetism, the young tend to idealize and emulate you, which enables you to be a potent influence for good in their lives.

In whatever area you utilize your special talents, your work methods are somewhat extreme. In other words, you can work like a beaver at times, putting in long hours, taking on work-loads that would stagger many another person. Then at other times (because you are basically a lion and not a beaver!) you can be extremely lazy, developing a great distaste for any form of labor, lying about indolently or dedicating yourself to the pursuit of pleasure. This lasts a bit and then it's back to the drawing board, with a renewed zest for work. This on-again, off-again mode of working can be very productive for you Leos, inasmuch as when you are putting out the effort it's as though you had the strength of ten; you can also play with equal intensity! Ideally, you would have your own profession or be otherwise self-employed, which would allow you to turn this hard-work, much-play polarity to your advantage. Those of you who are employed in nine-to-five jobs may have to discipline yourselves! Better yet, aim for the sort of job or career which will permit you to have the best of these two possible worlds.

All of your abilities and talents can, of course, be either used or neglected. While you are not exactly stubborn and you are not exactly lazy, you can give a pretty good imitation of both of these traits at times. You tend to become so self-involved, so wrapped up in your own ideas, desires, feelings, and reactions, that you never quite get past the periphery of your own ego. This can prompt you to dream big dreams, but never actually get around to realizing them. It's as though you were gazing into a mirror and loving the view, but common sense will tell you there's more to life than that! This is a negative example of Leo, but just in case it fits, take that one "giant step" over the rim of your self-absorption and into the mainstream of life, where you have a great deal to give and—in giving—to receive.

Both astrology and dreams are aids in helping you to realize your full potential. Pointed reminders pop up in dreams from time to time and can spotlight incidents in which you may have neglected an opportunity, or allowed a special ability or talent to go unexpressed. The imagery of the tawny lion sunning on a rock, lazily observing the action below, is picturesque and dramatic, too, when one realizes the great power of the beast. But when the lion descends from his lofty perch, that's when the action starts. In case you've not yet translated your own great strengths into concrete expression, your dreams may be reminding you that now is the time!

How Do You Dream? From a physical and visual standpoint, your dreams may take place in a king-size bed, possibly canopied and replete with satin sheets and elegant pillows. In fact, the question, How do you dream? does not refer to the setting of same, but to the quality and subject matter of your dreams. In general, your dreams would reflect your temperament by involving you in active, colorful episodes, fairly uncomplicated, and perhaps featuring you as the focal point in the dreams, with other people merely shadowy figures in the background. Most of us have numerous vague, disconnected, apparently meaningless dream episodes, and you are no exception. However, you should try to remember all your dreams, and by making the firm resolve to do so, just before falling asleep, you can train your conscious mind to receive and remember the subconscious messages of your dreams. Leos often tend to awaken in a rather irritable frame of mind (being a nocturnal person, morning hours are not your cup of tea at best). But one of the reasons for your irritability can be dreams that include lots of fussy little details, or confusions, or problems that are so minor you can't imagine why you would ever dream of them; for example, boxes that won't stay stacked, disarray in some room of the house, another person in your dream becoming disproportionately upset over a trifle, and so on. You do have a fine disdain of minor details in your waking hours, so that dreaming of, and becoming irritated by, such details in your dreams can be your subconscious reminding you that somewhere amidst the clutter there is one specific detail you should attend to. Because of your outgoing, forward-looking approach to life, you could be subject to frustration dreams at times. Also, with your fine sense of the dramatic, you are prone to dreams in which symbolism is featured.

What Specific Dream Categories Mean to You

Confinement Dreams This is the dream in which you are literally confined in some particular place from which you cannot escape. It may be a room, a closet, a house, or an unidentifiable place from which you try to exit, but can't. This sort of dream usually produces dream emotions of panic or fear. For a Leo, the dream reaction may be anger as you attempt with increasing force to push your way out. Sometimes the confinement dream is not so explicit. You may find yourself unable to move; a heaviness, almost a paralysis, of arms, legs, and even of your mental processes, sets in and there you are, confined in this vague way, for some vague purpose, and you don't like it a bit. Actually, the confinement dream represents a situation of your own making, probably in the recent past or currently operative. You've gotten yourself into a dilemma and you don't know how to get out of it. Perhaps this refers to a personal relationship, or a career condition, a family problem, or a financial bind. The confinement dream reflects your inability to act, to cope, or to resolve the matter. This is usually a "one-shot" type of dream, and as soon as in your conscious waking hours you do find the way out of your boxed-in situation, there is no reason to continue to dream about it. If you should have this type of dream frequently, it may represent a really serious, weighty situation in real life, which you are for some reason powerless to resolve. The clue in the confinement dream, though, is the fact that your powerlessness is self-imposed. Since you, in some way or another, got yourself into it—you do have the ability to get yourself out of it.

Insecurity Dreams No one escapes the insecurity dream, which sometimes features lost articles (usually purses, wallets, possessions, clothing, and so on) which you invariably do not find before you awaken—with the result that you face the day with feelings of worry, apprehension, or nervousness. This dream relates quite decidedly to a subconscious fear you have, nestled there in the back of your mind and not quite developed enough to be a matter that you focus on during your waking hours. It could refer to a tax write-off you took a chance on, which may or may not produce an audit (there's a fifty-fifty chance, so you're not really worried, but you're not really at ease about it, either). Or it could relate to your dealings with another, in which there is some basis for misunderstanding or accusation, but the other person has not as yet evidenced that sort of reaction (but you half expect he or she will do so). In other words, there is a situation in your waking life about which you have a shadowy fear; it's partially submerged, but not quite. So you dream this insecurity in a specific form—often the dream involves money or material possessions, simply because these are symbols of security for most people, though the basis of the dream need not be materialistic. Another reason for your insecurity dreams can stem from your Leonine self-assurance, only there is some area in your life about which you are not all that confident at the moment. This can be anything from sex to creative thinking, but the self-confident image you project in your waking hours may belie your subconscious insecurity about how you will follow through on some matter. An occasional insecurity dream is very normal; but if you have too many of them, your subconscious is pointing up the need for you to face up consciously to whatever you do feel insecure about—after which you can take the necessary steps to improve the situation. This, incidentally, is true of almost all dreams; so long as the underlying reason for the dream lies buried in your *sub*-conscious it will pop up in your dreams. Once recognized, brought into the light of day, faced up to, and acted upon, your subconscious has no further need to "nudge" you.

Frustration Dreams One of your nastier kinds of dreams! You Leos have very strong wills and anything that frustrates your firm intentions is bound to arouse your ire. When your "I will" meets up with a "but you can't," there goes the peace! This type of dream may consist of almost any kind of action or plot, but the key is that you are foiled in your expression of that "I will." Maybe you dream that you're held up (indefinitely) in traffic, or that you're going to meet someone who doesn't show. Or perhaps you start out in one dream episode, and before your intended action is performed you are transported into a completely different environment with your original plans unfulfilled. Or the frustration dream may concern a relationship; you must see someone who can't be found, or a person is just about to tell you something vital, when the scene changes or you wake up. The incompleted act is the keynote of the frustration dream, and this really upsets you. Whereas the confinement dream represents self-imposed restrictions, the frustration dream features "outside interference" as people fail you, or surroundings change unexpectedly, or some force or other intervenes to stop you short in whatever you were going to do. The message of this type of dream, for Leos, is your subconscious reminding you that you are not the center of the universe, that factors other than your own wishes and desires also must be taken into consideration. There may also be a clue here that you have not faced up to a frustrating condition in your waking life and so it shows up in your dreams in various guises.

Passive Dreams This is the type of dream which might be called a panorama—a series of pictures that unfold before your eyes. Even though you may be the featured performer in this "film," you do not, in your dream, fully participate in the action or in the dream reactions and emotions. You observe yourself going through your paces, but without much personal identification in the matter. These dreams are usually easier to remember, and even if the subject matter is happy or sad, you are not really elated or dejected by the plot. The reason for this type of dream stems from your need to be objective and impersonal about some waking-hours situation. For a Leo, especially, it offers you the opportunity to get outside of yourself, to view the matter impartially and without ego interference. The plot of the dream may in no way resemble the waking-hours situation (for such is the devious way in which our subconscious minds operate), but you will be able to identify it through the characters, conditions, or incidents in the dream episode, plus the general impression it leaves with you. If there are people in this dream, then the matter about which you should be more objective is a relationship. If you are the solo performer, then you need to be more detached in assessing your own abilities or judgment. If the dream plot is complicated, your subconscious is reminding you to evaluate carefully the details of a proposed course of waking-hours action.

Action Dreams You would like these dreams, particularly if the overall theme is pleasant, for this dream reflects your innate response to any sort of idea, dilemma, or proposal—which is, to take decisive action. In this sort of dream you may be walking, running, driving, skiing, swimming—any kind of action in which you can literally feel the ground beneath your feet, the air rushing by, the snow or water around you. It is a vital, aggressive type of dream, for you seem to experience fully the motion of your body. This dream correlates to decisive action you have recently taken or have resolved to take—it reinforces, so to speak, your mood of getting something done, settled, or started. In the event you are mulling over a real-life course of decisive action, this dream can be a forerunner of the affirmative action you are shortly to decide upon, your subconscious anticipating your firm resolve. Usually, this type of dream has beneficial results, for you awaken filled with the go-ahead spirit you Leos appreciate so well. In case the action dream is unpleasant or produces unpleasant dream results, your subconscious is pointing up possible hazards in your contemplated real-life action. Dreaming that you are whizzing down a ski slope, encountering a hidden boulder, and falling does not mean you're going to have an accident but merely that you should take into account the risks, hidden or otherwise, in your current action plan.

Recurring Dreams These are always important, for they mean your subconscious is drumming home a point to you and you are obviously not getting it. So the dream pops up now and again in reiterated fashion. This dream may repeat itself in exact detail, or it can be so similar in format and the impression it leaves with you that you get a feeling of déjà-vu. The recurring dream can relate to a waking-hours problem that needs to be worked out—a problem you either will not face or will not work on—or it can pinpoint some trait, habit, or orientation in yourself that needs attention. A simple example of the latter could be a dream in which you are going to do something (get up and sing or make a speech, or get married, or quit your job, or take a trip, or move), but before you get to the podium or altar or wherever, you walk out a door marked "Exit." This is your subconscious reminding you that there is something you should complete or follow up on (not necessarily related to the matter in the dream), perhaps a responsibility you're evading. Until you resolve the real-life condition (or overcome a certain negative trait of yours), you will probably experience the recurring dream from time to time. Your subconscious never gives up!

Escape Dreams Usually these are exhilarating dreams, and there should be more of them! In the escape dream you literally break free from a restrictive situation. You may walk out of a room, a house, your job, or someone's life. Or you may leap on a plane, train, bus, or into a car and take off for someplace much better than where you were. You have the feeling of having closed the door on a past problem or repressive situation, and obviously there is indeed some condition in your waking hours from which you would dearly love to escape. In this dream, your subconscious desire is realized in a concrete, identifiable manner. Actually, this sort of dream can set the stage for waking-hours action—not specifically mirroring the dream-episode activity, but which can put you in the mood to deal firmly and decisively with an obstacle or restrictive condition.

Sex Dreams Basically, the more active and satisfying your waking-hours sex life, the less you will tend to experience the sex dream. As the sex drive is one of the strongest drives, it is less easily diverted or sublimated and will remain a potent subconscious desire which shows up in your dreams. Leos not only have good, healthy sex drives, but often their expressing of sexual needs—and particularly their sexual attraction for others—is tied in with their overall self-confidence. This is, of course, true of many people, but especially of Leos. Tell a Leo he or she is not sexy and you've lost a friend! Accordingly, you may experience sex dreams when for some reason you are not given the credit, respect, or admiration you feel is due you in some other, unrelated area of life. It is your subconscious reaffirming your faith in yourself, and doing it in a sexual way because this is part and parcel of your entire self-esteem. Very rarely are the sex partners in people's dreams those individuals most desired in real life. However, the person with whom you suddenly find yourself sharing sexual pleasures in your dream may represent an image or a sex symbol to you. There may be a resemblance to someone you sexually desire; or the age, professional status, or life style of the dream partner may be identifiable as a symbol of one you'd really like to have in your arms.

Sensuous Dreams These are not necessarily sexual, but relate to the senses of sight, hearing, smell, taste, and touch. In this sort of dream the sense reaction is very real; you seem to actually hear the music, or see the colors, or taste the food, and so on. Leos are appreciative of sensuous pleasures, and when this type of dream is a pleasant one, it merely reflects your basic appreciation of life. Specifically, it can echo a recent or about-to-happen event of an enjoyable nature: a party, trip, promotion, perhaps a little financial bonanza which you intend spending on an item that will give you sense pleasure, for example, an oil painting, opera ticket, a gourmet dinner, or a gorgeous gown. If anyone loves the good things in life, you do, so your sensuous dream, when pleasant, is your subconscious pampering your various sense appreciations. On the other hand, if the sensuous dream is unpleasant, such as your hearing discordant music, smelling a bad odor, overeating to the point of indigestion, your subconscious is saying, watch it! You are, in waking hours, overdoing some form of sensuous self-indulgence and could soon be reminded that he who dances must pay the piper!

Precognitive Dreams This is the dream in which

either the next day or some days later the events of the dream are mirrored in an actual happening; or, the general theme or impression of the dream is duplicated when a real-life event produces the same impression and reactions. Your subconscious can often be a step ahead of you and in the precognitive dream can give you a "glimpse of the future," which, of course, you do not usually recognize until subsequent events confirm it. Sometimes, though, the sense of foreboding or anticipation is so strong upon awakening that you are convinced the dream has a special meaning. The general-impression type of precognitive dream might involve, for example, your dreaming that a deceased relative is talking with your son or daughter, and your foreboding may concern a fear that the child will die. In actuality, the next day's mail may produce a letter of rejection from the college of his or her choice—an unfortunate happening, certainly, but not fatal. In other words, the theme of foreboding may later be mirrored in an unpleasant incident but not as unpleasant as you feared. If the precognitive dream is duplicated in exact detail by a subsequent event, for the most part such a dream-and-reality event does not seem all that important. You may dream that you went to the supermarket and ran into a former neighbor, and lo and behold, the next day you do. That sort of thing. The value in this kind of exact duplication dream is that your subconscious is letting you know that you do have some sort of extrasensory ability, that such an inexplicable thing as a dream preceding the actual event is proof positive that there is more to life than material matters, and that maybe you should spend a little more time and thought on spiritual or occult interests. As a Leo, you have a direct channel to spiritual guidance. That many Leos are not particularly prone to the precognitive dream simply means that they are intensely occupied with enjoying the here and now and may not allow time for reflection, meditation, and other introspective pursuits.

Peopled Dreams You would tend to dream of people in crowds, throngs, groups, in which the faces are unidentifiable. Or you will dream of yourself and one other individual, in some sort of one-to-one situation. Although you care for people in a general way—wishing humanity well, so to speak—you're not really that concerned with individuals and their problems, ideas, or conversation, except those specific individuals who are your family, close friends, or loved ones. As a result, you are not conditioned by your waking hours to dream of people in terms of what they really are as individuals (with the above exceptions) but merely as a backdrop for your own dream activities. Public opinion means a lot to you Leos, not so much in terms of worrying what people will think (basically you don't really care what "they" think), but in terms of your own image and the respect, esteem, or admiration you feel is due that image. People in general, are, in fact, your audience, both in dreams and in real life. If, in your dreams, these "background" people are generally approving, your subconscious is pointing up the fact that at least in the public area of your life, all goes well. If they are hostile or if they *ignore* you, then you have a subconscious concern that you are not projecting your image as you wish it to be seen, or maybe you are not projecting yourself enough, for Leos were never meant to blush unseen, like the violet!

Symbols in Dreams Dreams contain a lot of symbolism, whereby an object or person in your dream may represent (i.e., be a symbol of) something else, but once in a while you may dream of a subject that is especially symbolic: a number, perhaps, or a certain color, an animal, abstract sign, maybe an element (fire, earth, air, or water). The elements have astrological meaning. Fire represents the spirit; earth, the material body; air, the mind; and water, the emotions. The element of fire is particularly symbolic for you, as yours is a fire sign. Fire also represents spiritual awakening; a dream of fire in which you experience feelings of personal danger would signify your subconscious spotlighting your need for more spiritual awareness, or possibly that your spiritual faith was being endangered by some habit or condition in your life. On the other hand, fire that is pleasing and controlled, such as a cozy fireplace or a lit candle, would show good balance between your spiritual principles and your general life style. A dream involving the element of air (flying, breathing in fresh, pure, country air, feeling the air rush past you in the course of some speed sport) denotes your expanding mind power. Fire-related dreams and air-related dreams, unless very unpleasant, are compatible with your temperament and show that your subconscious is "pointing" you in the right direction for realizing your spiritual and mental potential. Dreaming of an animal will be symbolic in terms of what the animal means to *you*; if you are fond of pets, dreaming of one can be a love symbol, but if you dislike or fear animals, dreaming of one can mean you're uneasy or suspicious of someone's actions or motives. If you should dream of the numbers one or eight, the color gold (or a golden object), or of a Lion, that dream will be significant. Your subconscious reveals, through symbolism, your true identity, perhaps what your life goals should be, so seek the inner meaning of the dream.

Chapter 9

Virgo

(August 24—September 23)

Your most natural instincts arise from your unconscious, while your deepest desires (which are very often submerged to the point where you are not aware of them) are in the realm of your subconscious. Your Sun sign represents the essence of your own unique individuality, the filter, so to speak, through which your unconscious instincts and subconscious desires are expressed. Because you are a Virgo, your dreams reflect this individuality in their content and meaning.

VIRGO is an Earth sign, ruled by Mercury, mutable in quality (which means adaptable and flexible). The combination of the earth element and the mutability of your sign is shown in your temperament, for you are practical, logical, objective in your thinking, and have a certain aptitude for "making do" with whatever the conditions or circumstances in which you may find yourself. Your cerebral orientation stems from the planet Mercury, which not only represents mind power but is related to all forms of communications and to transportation as well. Accordingly, you often gravitate toward a life style which includes quite a bit of running to and fro (Mercury is the "celestial messenger" in mythology) and frequently toward a job or career in communications: advertising, writing, teaching, selling, acting, or public speaking. Virgo's description as the sign of service also orients you toward helping others, a humanitarianism that may propel you toward a career in medicine, education, or social service, or—in your personal life—toward rendering practical forms of "service" to family, friends, and in your group affiliations. You Virgos are frequently the ones who wind up doing all those little nitty-gritty chores which others often avoid! The earth element of your sign is evident in your good sense of material values, while your flair for handling details, figures, records, and lists reflects that sense of orderliness which is so much a part of Virgo. Whether by design or accident, you are the one who, in the family circle, keeps track of expenditures, household necessities, and remembers who's due for a dental or medical check-up and when. In your career surroundings, you're the one who always finishes up the day's work and leaves a tidy desk; and in social group situations, it's you who makes sure enough food has been ordered, who efficiently does the chores that others forget (including last-minute emergencics, like obtaining two-dozen extra chairs!).

Your Unconscious Instincts You have strong urges to analyze and to create order, the second being a logical outcome of the first. And speaking of logic, this too is a medium in which you instinctively operate. A leads to B, B leads to C, C leads to D, and you will have it no other way. Mr. Spock of Star Trek fame must surely be a Virgo, for his "that is the *logical* thing to do" reflects the calm, dispassionate objectivity of Virgo. Your urge to analyze is the cornerstone of your success in life, for you separate all things into simple, functional components, line them up in their proper, orderly sequence, then utilize them logically and efficiently. This applies to your handling of problems, your work methods, your beliefs, principles, and ethics, and your approach to the big goals in your life. The only area in which this technique sometimes fails you is in personal relationships—people being frequently unpredictable and certainly not always logical! While a person's subconscious desires and conscious aims and interests can modify and often complicate the basic unconscious instincts, still, the individual is happiest and most fulfilled when at least some part of these unconscious instincts can be operative. As a Virgo, you should never be forced into a mold where chaos and confusion are the order of the day. Because of your adaptable, flexible nature you would be inclined to remain in that mold, making the best of it, but being extremely miserable and nervous as a result. This would apply to a job or career environment where everything was done in a hit-or-miss fashion and no one ever knew where anything was kept; to a residential situation where you had absolutely no privacy (*essential* for a Virgo) and where loud voices, arguments, or three transistor radios blended with a CB radio to create the din of dins; or to a personal relationship in which the other person was lazy, sloppy, moody, short-tempered, and illogical. In other words, you should not deny your basic instincts for orderliness, logic, and privacy by getting into chaotic situations.

Hopefully, you have high goals in life—important plans and interests. However, it is a Virgo failing to be self-limiting, and this, too, stems from that unconscious instinct to analyze. You analyze yourself, your abilities, and your talents as objectively as you analyze objects, conditions, or other people, with the result that you sometimes feel you are not really equipped for big things. Actually, Virgo, you should be a bit more prejudiced in your own behalf! Unconscious instincts can be recognized, nurtured, directed into positive expression (even improved upon when necessary) by an act of the conscious will. These unconscious instincts are constantly operative, awake or asleep, forming a backdrop to your dreams. However, the majority of your dreams are produced by . . .

Your Subconscious Desires Subconsciously, you wish to make life more perfect and to help others—or it could be the other way around. Goodness knows, you've been called a perfectionist often enough, Virgo, and have been reminded that yours is indeed the sign of service. As with the unconscious instincts and subconscious desires of all signs of the Zodiac, these specific qualities can be expressed positively or negatively. For Virgos, negative expression of your desires to make life more perfect and to help others can mean you nag your nearest and dearest to be cleaner, neater, smarter, or more quiet, polite, or well organized than *they* have any desire to be (or the capacity to be, for that matter). You do this to help them and to create a more perfect environment. Or, still on the negative theme, you may have a fit if someone moves a book or ashtray, thereby disturbing an orderly arrangement. That is, assuming you *have* an ashtray, which is a dirt-producing little object at best; by not encouraging people to smoke you are helping them. You get the picture: some not particularly attractive things that you do with the best of intentions. Heaven knows there is certainly room for more order in life, more striving for perfection; and there is certainly a need for helpfulness. So Virgo's *positive* expression of subconscious desires could actually make a difference globally, if directed in the proper channels. Service to humanity is the noblest of objectives, through which many can be helped and their lives made, if not perfect, at least considerably better. It is a waste when Virgos get bogged down with small perfectionisms and limited forms of service, when their potential is so very great—greater than most Virgos realize.

In your personal, professional, and social life, as well as in your group affiliations, you always seek to improve procedures or to clear up messy situations of one sort or another. You'll be the one who reorganizes the filing systems or catalogs at work, from which all benefit in the long run; you are the one who takes over an organization's books (after the previous treasurer, who made no entries for months, took off for parts unknown with what was left of the petty cash). You'll see to the family's nutrition, laundry, and domestic needs, while keeping after the kids to do their homework and after your mate to complete various jobs he or she started. But while all of this is helpful and contributes to your desire to make life more perfect, still you often do feel unappreciated, or at least taken for granted—which is indeed sometimes the case. An interesting continuity in the Zodiac very often produces signs that are diametrically opposed to each other as in the case of gentle Pisces being succeeded by aggressive Aries, or slow, steady Taurus being succeeded by quick, flighty Gemini. Virgo succeeds Leo in the Zodiac, and whereas Leo in general is quick to claim attention, praise, and the limelight, you Virgos tend to shrink from pushing yourselves forward at all. You don't "blow your own horn" or demand attention and compliments, which is why you sometimes *are* taken for granted. But deep in your subconscious, along with the desire to make life more perfect and to help others, is a conviction that *logically* people should recognize your value and give you the credit and appreciation due you. This can show up in your dreams in a disturbing way, when you experience frustration and insecurity dreams, though there may be the occasional bonus of a really enjoyable escape dream, in which you simply fly away from responsibilities (and those who take you for granted!). For Virgos, especially, learning to pinpoint the meanings of such dreams can be invaluable, for once you recognize the source of your frustration or insecurity, it becomes much easier to turn things around a bit in your waking life so that you can maximize the joy of giving—and also maximize the deserved credit you receive for it!

Your Special Abilities and Talents These are in the realm of your conscious state, your waking-hours awareness. You are undoubtedly cognizant of some of your special talents, such as your ability to hold to practical standards in material matters, even when faced with the temptation to spend and spend. There is also your ability to "keep your head when those about you are losing theirs," and the way you stay on an even keel in matters of duty and responsibility, where you are ultrareliable, ultradependable. You also have the ability to learn, which not everyone has. In fact, you are somewhat the eternal student, very much attracted to taking various courses and perhaps even more inclined to self-education via reading. You Virgos are all great readers, and as soon as you left your baby carriage you probably crawled straight to the bookcase and reached for the handiest tome.

Another of your special abilities is indeed a rare one: the ability to be totally objective in your thinking, unswayed by emotionalism or subjective, personal interests. This is not only because you are mentally polarized, but also because you have a good control of your emotions. As the majority of people do not think with their minds, but with their emotions or from some personal bias, you stand out as a true intellectual (in the sense that it's your fair, impartial intellect that prevails over emotionalism). Your ability to discriminate—to compare, judge, and select—stems from your unconscious instinct to analyze. This is what, on an everyday level, makes you a super shopper; in your career, one who determines top priorities and gets them done first; and in your personal life, someone who adheres to high principles and certain modes of behavior. You Virgos are often told that you are overly critical, but your criticism, far from being negative or destructive, is merely the verbalization of your mental processes. You analyze, discriminate, and then make your comment ("I like your blue dress better than that one," or "Your drapes need to be cleaned," or "I see you haven't weeded your garden lately," and so on). True, your verbalizations of this analyze-discriminate pattern sometimes have an adverse effect, as others accuse you of being hypercritical or nit-picking, but that's simply because you may not have learned diplomacy (it's not what you say, it's how you say it!).

Regarding your talents, they are certainly plentiful—or can be, once you allow yourself that easy flow in which action follows inspiration without being endlessly filtered through the analyzing process. Mercury, your sign ruler, gives you a special affinity for working with words (writing, teaching, speaking), and also for work done with the hands, such as sculpting, painting, and various forms of handiwork. You are adept in the use of the typewriter and other office machines, and in taking dictation. Your affinity for books gives you a special talent as librarian or curator of a rare-book collection. Music is another of your talents (or potential talents), and the piano could be your number-one instrument. You have natural rhythm and would be attracted to the intricacies of musical composition and the precision required to play an instrument.

All of your abilities and talents can, of course, either be used or neglected. Sometimes you lack that certain aggressiveness that's needed to promote yourself and your talents; or it may be that you are inwardly a bit timid about exposing yourself to possible failure. Being a reserved, somewhat shy individual, you do have a horror of "public" failure, of falling flat on your face where all the world can see. You also have a slight fear of the unknown. You are a person who likes to know where you are, wbere you're going, and how you're going to get there, with all the details filled in. This is where you can be at a disadvantage, because it's impossible to predict in advance such variables as other people's reactions and whether or not the scene as you envision it will turn out to be precisely *as* you envision it. In other words, Virgo, you have got to learn to take a chance, and to use that fine objective mind of yours to realize that even if you should make a mess of your first try at something big, "the world will little note nor long remember" your humiliation. So, you simply pick yourself up, dust yourself off, and try once more! If you are in this category of Virgos who want to do more than they're doing, to utilize talents to the fullest, yet are timid, hesitant, reluctant, or fearful of taking that first step, your dreams will surely reflect your frustration. Confinement dreams, in which the confinement is indeed self-imposed because you are the only one who can break through the barriers, or frustration or insecurity dreams, in which actions are incompleted or you are nervously uneasy because you cannot find something, all stem from your subconscious. It is reminding you that your desire to make life more perfect should also include the fulfillment of your own potential, and that maybe your desire to be helpful should be focused on yourself once in a while.

Take a moment to review your life to date, to see where you may have missed out because you held back, feeling inadequate, unprepared, or unsure of yourself. You might also take a look around you and see all the people in top positions or leading interesting life styles who basically are far less knowledgable or talented than you, but are quite a bit more "pushy," which should tell you something! It may have been a job promotion you sidestepped because you felt unequipped to handle it or a personal relationship in which you were a bit too reserved, or too shy, or perhaps you retreated in the face of competition. Somewhere along the line you might have flubbed it, not because you were inadequate, but because you did not make a spontaneous, enthusiastic response to opportunity. Your dreams may be reminding you of these same situations.

How Do You Dream? Aside from the fact that this question refers to the context and meanings of your dreams, and not to your sleeping environment (Virgos, however, do tend to sleep all bunched up in the fetal position), it should also be pointed out that you are among those who really require a good night's sleep—whether six, eight, or ten hours are your particular need. Basically healthy, you do have a finely tuned nervous system as well as a somewhat sensitive digestive tract, so proper (and preferably plain) food and sufficient sleep time are a must if you are to be in peak physical condition. As to the contents of your dreams, if you find it difficult to remember dream sequences, you of all people—with your excellent mental capabilities—can "train" your mind to remember. Make a firm resolution to do so, just prior to falling asleep. Your dreams tend to come in segments, often short self-contained units, with many subjects being covered in one night's dream episodes. You will often find yourself feeling baffled in a dream, unable to cope, make a decision, or get your message across to others. Action dreams would be exhilarating to you, as would your occasional escape dream; but you may experience a preponderance of confinement, frustration, or insecurity dreams, which will surely diminish in frequency the more you consciously face up to problems (self-imposed or otherwise) and take decisive action concerning them.

What Specific Dream Categories Mean to You

Confinement Dreams These are the dreams in which you are locked in somewhere. Having gotten in, you cannot get out. Or perhaps you are unable to move your limbs or even utter a cry. Sometimes in this sort of dream there is also a sense of vague, unidentified danger. Although this is an unpleasant kind of dream episode, it does not always mean specifically what it seems to mean. This dream is not a forerunner of your being confined per se, but represents a condition in your life that, quite literally, confines you. It may be a responsibility or burden, but the key to this dream is that your confinement stems from your own actions—or lack of action. The responsibility or burden, for example, can be unloaded or lightened; depending on some action that *you* can take. Or perhaps you have committed yourself to a certain course of action and are now having second thoughts about it. The dream places you in a confinement situation as a reminder that you got yourself into this difficulty and that you can get yourself out of it! Because you are a Virgo and exceptionally scrupulous about honoring commitments and fulfilling obligations, you might be likely to experience this sort of dream. (You would also be smart to think twice before accepting added obligations!)

Insecurity Dreams Inasmuch as security means a lot to you, this type of dream would be disturbing—especially as it often features the loss of some material object (for example, a purse, wallet, car, or clothing). Although you are not materialistic to the extent that money or possessions are your number-one priority, still, material security does play a large role in your life, and can, in fact, sometimes mean the difference between your feeling confident or fearful. When you awaken from an insecurity dream, you would tend to experience an unsettled feeling. In this sort of dream, something on which you very much depend is lost or missing. Money being something we all depend on, purses and wallets are among the most common missing articles in dreams. Actually, the money is symbolic, as this sort of dream can reflect emotional insecurity as well as material insecurity in waking hours. A relationship that's not going too well (you may fear that you will "lose" this person), or someone you care for who tends to be irresponsible or unreliable, may be the actual source of the lost-purse-or-wallet dream. Loss of clothing in a dream is symbolic of a feared loss of self-esteem or status and an apprehension that you may be "exposed" as being undignified, dishonest, immoral, somehow unworthy. The insecurity dream (by far the most prevalent among dream categories) very often stems from a really minor incident about which you may subconsciously feel a disproportionate sense of guilt. An inadvertent "social snub" to a friend, for instance, could produce the lost-article dream (you fear the loss of this friendship); or perhaps you indulged in a shady action (someone forgot their change and you didn't remind them), and your dream of arriving nude at a dinner party is the subconscious guilt compounded by the fear that your small dishonesty will be publicized. Everyone has insecurity dreams, but if you have them frequently, it can mean that you are doing lots of little "unworthy" things about which you are nervously apprehensive—or that you are over scrupulous and attach far too much importance to really minor incidents. In either case, self-analysis can be the antidote.

Frustration Dreams You are rather prone to this type of dream, inasmuch as you Virgos tend to put up with a great deal before you rebel. When you do, however, it's "the last straw" type of situation and a tiny incident can set off a tantrum. Consequently, everyone is very critical that you should get so upset over a trifle. The frustration dream, however, represents all those accumulated irritating incidents over which you did not blow up. Instead, you relegated all the fuming and fulminating to your subconscious—where they show up in dreams. In the frustration dream you are usually unable to complete whatever it is you set out to do. You're going to see a person who isn't there, or are taking a bus that just left, or it can carry over into the sex dream, where the sex act is incompleted. The frustration dream can be in two or more episodes. You have a specific objective in the first, then the scene changes and you're left with the nagging feeling that there was "something" you should have done but didn't. Your frustration dreams can provide clues to real-life situations or people that frustrate you. This can be helpful, for very often you are unaware in waking hours of the *real* source of your frustration. Once recognized, frustration is easier to handle, especially for a Virgo with your fine analytical flair.

Passive Dreams This can be a most helpful kind of dream for you, as it enables you to get the "big picture" and keeps you from getting overly involved with the nonessentials (which Virgos sometimes tend to do). In the passive dream, you observe but do not participate. Instead of experiencing the dream action, whatever it may be, you watch yourself proceeding along in the plot of the dream. You usually do not experience the emotions or reactions that you would in a dream in which you actually participate, but view it all as on a film or TV screen. The object of this sort of dream is for your subconscious to provide you with the overview. While you Virgos are certainly capable of a fine objective, detached attitude, you are prone (in your waking hours) to getting hung up occasionally on some small detail that's really not germane to the "plot." So this dream presents you with the total panorama, from which you should be able to identify persons, situations, events of the recent past or currently in operation, and achieve a more balanced and comprehensive perspective.

Action Dreams Most dreams have some sort of action in them but this dream produces action that is much more vividly experienced. You may be walking, running, playing golf, tennis, or whatever, and it is so real that you can actually feel the ground beneath your feet, or the golf club or tennis racquet in your hand. Often there is also a sense of urgency in this sort of dream; you must get somewhere quickly, so you run; or you are being chased, so you jump and leap. If the action dream is pleasant, this represents quite literally that you have taken decisive action about a real-life situation, or have made a firm decision to do so in the immediate future. Your subconscious is showing you the joy of being action-oriented (as opposed to mulling over problems or worrying). If the dream is unpleasant such as your being pursued by someone with evil intent, or your rushing about nervously with no sense of direction, then your subconscious is pointing up the fact that a recent move you made, or one you propose to make, could merit further thought, maybe more preparation.

Recurring Dreams These are always significant for they concern a specific matter about which your subconscious keeps repeating the "message." Sometimes recurring dreams are years apart, sometimes more frequent. They may be exact repeats, or merely have a similar theme. Obviously, they refer to a problem that needs to be resolved, a condition that requires change or revision, or perhaps something in yourself—a trait or attitude—that could stand a bit of working on. Remembering that dreams are frequently clothed in symbolism, try to get to the real meaning of your recurring dreams. For instance, you may have a recurring dream about a specific person, but this person may not be at all involved in your problem, serving rather as an "image" of the essential matter. For example, dreaming of your boss could refer to a parental problem, with your boss representing the authority figure or father image; or dreaming of a long-lost romance could really be a clue to your difficulty in a current relationship. Until you identify and consciously work on the subject matter of your recurring dreams, they will keep popping up.

Escape Dreams Any dream in which you leave behind something unpleasant or worrying for something enjoyable and relaxing is an escape dream. Sometimes this sort of dream is delightfully specific: You emerge from dank, dark shadows into sunshine, blue skies, and grassy turf; or you leap into a plane, train, or bus and take off joyously for pleasure travel; or perhaps you slam the door on antagonisms and dissensions and step into a brand new environment. Everyone has some burdens or responsibilities and everyone has the desire for freedom, to a greater or lesser extent. The escape dream satisfies the craving for a carefree, mobile life, and you'll usually find that you awaken after such a dream filled with zest, ambition, and optimism. The basic meaning of this dream is that you would like to be more free, and your subconscious is providing at least the dream opportunity for it. By all rights, people who are heavily burdened in waking hours really should experience the escape dream more often, but this does not seem to be the case. The escape dream is more in the nature of a "safety valve" opened by your subconscious when you most need to let off steam.

Sex Dreams Virgos, who are often underestimated in terms of their sexual interest and prowess, tend to experience sex dreams no more or less often than anyone else. Invariably, the more active and fulfilling your actual sexual experiences are, the less need there will be for you to dream of sex. Since the sex drive is one of the strongest, repression of it in waking hours can divert it into dream episodes, sometimes with surprising partners or in unlikely situations! (This can be very embarrassing to a Virgo, whose sense of propriety is very strong, even in a dream.) Sometimes Virgo people do tend to become involved in real-life impossible love situations, where one or both individuals are not free, or the Virgo's love is not reciprocated, or there develops an almost obsessive attraction for an individual the Virgo has never even met. This sort of emotional involvement is not, for one reason or another, expressed sexually. In this kind of situation, you will tend to have frequent sex dreams, though seldom with the partner on whom your love is actually focused. Of course everyone's life style, opportunities, standards, and preferences are different, but generally speaking, having too many sex dreams is not particularly healthy (in terms of mental and emotional health), for they are merely substitutions for the real thing. They can also lead to a waking-hours preoccupation with the subject, upsetting the balance of perspective.

Sensuous Dreams This sort of dream is not necessarily sex oriented, but rather involves the senses of sight, hearing, smell, taste, and touch. In the sensuous dreams these sense experiences are very vivid, with colors clearer and sharper, sounds definite and identifiable, scents extremely pronounced, foods really affecting your taste buds, and tactile experience very specific (really smooth satins and rough woollens). The meaning of these dreams depends on whether the sense experiences are pleasant or unpleasant. If enjoyable, then your subconscious is savoring, so to speak, a recent pleasant event (not necessarily related to the subject of the dream, but of a material, worldly nature—a financial windfall, flattering publicity, a social triumph). If the sensuous dream is unpleasant—the music harsh, the odor repellent, the colors clashing, or the food sickening—then your subconscious is pointing up the need for restraint. You may be overindulging one of your appetites, though not necessarily the one featured in the dream. For Virgos, this type of dream also has a creative meaning, as enjoyable sense experiences stem from your subconscious heightening your appreciation of color, sound, or beauty, and awakening your urge to create the same.

Precognitive Dreams You could be inclined to have precognitive dreams, provided you do not shut them out through *too* much common sense or practicality of the "it's-only-a-coincidence" variety. Actually, Virgos can be very much tuned in to the spiritual realm, and the precognitive dream, in which dream events are repeated in an actual happening shortly after the dream occurs, is but one of the links to the spiritual level. Other precognitive dreams come to actuality in essence if not in detail. You might dream, for example, that you are joyously dancing at a friend's wedding, and the subsequent event will be the receipt of good news, or an enjoyable social occasion. Or the news of someone's death, which you receive in your dream, may manifest in another type of loss soon to occur (money, a possession, a broken friendship). One does not always realize that a precognitive dream has occurred until later events prove it out. But, generally speaking, this type of dream stems from your subconscious providing a glimpse of the future—providing a glimpse, as well, of your own psychic ability, intuition, or spiritual potential.

Peopled Dreams Virgos are inclined to dream of many individuals, for although yours is a sign in which privacy and solitude are among the keynotes—and are most necessary for you to have from time to time, in order to think, reflect, and recharge your energies—you are very much others-oriented. You have that innate desire to be helpful to others, and you are also rather conscious of the impression you make on others, sometimes even being subject to the "what-will-people-think?" attitude. So, your awareness of other people being twofold, you will be inclined to experience peopled dreams. In fact, just as you are falling asleep, many faces may parade by your dream view, mostly faces of strangers. Then as you fall more deeply into sleep, the dream episodes feature groups or crowds of people, sometimes as a backdrop to your own dream activities, sometimes as part of the action. Communications may be featured in your peopled dreams; you're giving someone news or information, or you're trying to get your ideas across; or someone is calling you (Virgos often hear their names called loudly in dreams), and this relates significantly to your establishing your real identity. These peopled dreams can also be symbolic, for the people in your dreams are not necessarily the ones of real importance in your life. The group or crowd can be symbolic of your attitude toward your status and reputation; or the individuals could be "images" of certain others (a woman in your dream may be the principal female in your life; mother, sister, wife, etc.). Comments made by individuals in your peopled dreams can be significant when related to real-life situations.

Symbols in Dreams As previously mentioned, dreams are fraught with symbolism, and as you learn to identify the symbols and relate them to people and conditions in your life you will find that your subconscious is truly aiding you in self-understanding. However, there are also dreams in which especially symbolic objects appear, such as an animal, a certain numeral, an impressive design or abstract pattern, maybe an element—fire, earth, air, or water—or nature objects, such as trees, flowers, stones, and so on. The elements are significant, astrologically, as fire represents the spirit, earth the material body, air the mind, and water the emotions. The element of earth is particularly meaningful for you, for yours is an earth sign; a dream involving earthy matters—meadows, mountains, gardens, or agricultural produce—can mean (if it is a pleasant dream) a reaffirmation of your identity, your basic beliefs and principles. An unpleasant earth dream is your subconscious reminding you to hold fast to basic principles, to your essential individuality. Earth-related and water-related dreams are compatible with your temperament and represent an "encouraging word" to press on toward realization of your full potential. Dreaming of an animal will be symbolic in terms of what the animal means to *you*: If you like domestic animals, pets (and you should, as Virgo rules small animals), then to dream of one can mean friendship, a love object, or other relationship-oriented pleasure. In case you do not care for animals, dreaming of one can represent a worry, a fear, or a suspicion currently occupying your subconscious mind. If you should dream of the number seven, the color blue, or of a sheaf of grain used in making "our daily bread," this dream will be significant. The symbol of Virgo is a virgin holding the sheaf of wheat—symbolic of potential motherhood, nourishment, service—and your subconscious would be pinpointing, through symbolism, your true identity and potential, even the direction your life is to take for your greatest fulfillment.

Chapter 10

Libra

(September 24–October 23)

Your unconscious state is the realm of your natural instincts; your subconscious is the source of your deepest desires, often so deeply buried that you are unaware of them. Your Sun sign might be termed the "packaging" through which your unconscious and subconscious operate, for this represents your own individuality. Because you are a Libran, your dreams are highly personalized and reflect your unconscious and subconscious states.

LIBRA is an air sign, ruled by Venus, cardinal in quality (which means action-oriented). The blend of the air element and the cardinality of your sign is expressed through your temperament, for you are ever alert to opportunities to better yourself, to move on to higher levels. The higher levels you naturally are drawn to almost always include some of those ingredients that are inherent in the "good life"; luxuries, comforts, elegance, cultural pleasures, and of course romantic pleasures, for Libra's association with Venus highlights its role as the planet of love and beauty. The air element inclines you to interests in music, art, literature, fashion; this, plus the Venus influence, gives you a keen appreciation of beauty—in others as well as in yourself (Librans are frequently beautiful, or if not, they achieve an "aura" of beauty via fashion, cosmetics, impeccable taste). Cardinal-sign people tend to be opportunists, which, in a positive way, simply means spotting opportunity nearly everywhere and immediately making the most of it. Opportunism expressed in your special Venusian style, prompts you to be subtle and diplomatic in your manner, but you forge ahead nevertheless. Because Libra is the sign of relationships, other people are important in your life and you are happiest and most fulfilled when living and working with another toward mutual goals. That Venusian love-and-romance pattern strongly inclines you toward marriage and other meaningful relationships. Librans tend to marry early and often! But due to your orientation toward romance, comforts, and luxuries, sometimes the everyday responsibilities of marriage and the less glamorous aspects of it all are disillusioning to you. Ideally, Librans should have a glamorously exciting career (or be married to someone with a glamorously exciting career) and have enough money to employ others to do the housework, tend to boring chores, and take care of the children!

Your Unconscious Instincts You have strong urges to balance and to relate. These are echoed in the symbol of your sign, the Scales, and to your ruling planet, Venus, the relationship instigator par excellence. Many of your actions and objectives stem from these unconscious instincts, which is why, when you are faced with a choice between two courses of action, or a decision to be made, you do not impulsively make your choice or decision, but instead consider all angles to the matter, mull over all possible alternatives, weigh the pros and cons (in keeping with the symbolic Scales). In fact, you've probably been pressured a bit on occasion by more impatient types who want you to make up your mind. True, your tendency to deliberate can be negatively expressed for you can indeed be a fence sitter, *never* taking a stand or making a decision. Or you can vacillate—making your choices and decisions, then changing them, back and forth like a pendulum. However, these are negative examples and, as a general rule, you should not allow yourself to be pressured by those seeking speedy action. You will exercise much better judgment *after* you consider all the pros and cons (within a reasonable time, naturally).

Your unconscious urge to relate has both personal and impersonal connotations. As previously stated, Libra is the sign of relationships (marriage, partnership, collaboration), and on a strictly personal level, you are in your element when indulging in Venusian flirtatiousness! While you *can* be self-sufficient if you absolutely have to be, your natural bent is to team up with another, in both personal or professional relationships. In a broader context, though, your urge to relate is expressed through bringing others together. You tend to mediate when there are differences of opinion, bringing opposing forces together on some sort of common ground for agreement. You can do this wonderfully well, whether on a personal level, bringing two feuding friends together, or in your professional capacity, mediating between management and labor, being a troubleshooter and seeing to it that just grievances get heard. Many a Libran is also involved in diplomatic work in government and industry, for you have the delightful talent for being able to maintain friendly relations, with diametrically opposed factions while working to get them both to sit down at the peace table. This is where your noted tact, diplomacy, and charm come in very handy! In general, your unconscious urges to balance and to relate result in positive expression. Once in a while there pops up a really negative Libran who is not only vacillating and unreliable, but who perversely diverts the urge to relate into the urge to agitate, a counterproductive expression that results in his or her making trouble between others instead of making peace. Unconscious instincts can be recognized, nurtured, and directed into positive expression; for they are constantly operative, forming a backdrop to your dreams. However, the majority of your dreams are produced by . . .

Your Subconscious Desires Subconsciously, you wish for companionship and for pleasure. The desire for companionship stems from your unconscious urge to relate, while your desire for pleasure is strictly from Venus! These desires are apparent in your waking hours in your natural gravitation toward social and/or romantic relationships and toward all of life's little luxuries that you can get your hands on! You tend to be fashion-conscious, attracted to "in" places for dining and entertainment. You simply adore things like minks, chinchillas, Rolls Royces, and cruises to the Greek Isles, and unless you are totally dedicated to antiestablishment, antitradition attitudes, your favorite fantasy of yourself would go something like this: You're wearing a fabulous original, dining in the most elegant and expensive restaurant, complete with candlelight, vintage wine, violin music, and facing the most handsome/beautiful love partner in the world, who murmurs many a compliment and many a sweet nothing during the course of the evening. In other words, you are exceedingly attracted to glamour and romance, and also to the glamour *of* romance.

There is also another aspect to Venus, your ruling planet, which sometimes gets overlooked. Venus represents money as well as love and, in your case, Libra, it takes a lot of money to keep you in the style to which you would like to become accustomed! However, if need be, you can be quite successful in handling any financial situation, for you have a natural flair for spotting an opportunity and subtly but effectively following up on it. Frequently, you can do well in a business/financial partnership, particularly of the kind where one partner has specific practical, behind-the-scenes functions, while the other (you) are the front man or woman, handling the firm's image, its public relations in the sort of business deals that are conducted on the country club golf course, or at some millionaire's social soiree.

Whatever your career or goals in life, your ultimate aim will be to achieve a position in which you can realize your deep desires for companionship and pleasure. You could be a world leader, a dedicated scientist or humanitarian, or a brilliantly creative person, but somewhere in the midst of your hectic pace of activity, you manage to set time aside for "gracious living."

In your dreams, whether they are clear-cut or vague and shadowy, your subconscious desires are being revealed. Invariably they will tie in with relationships (general or specific) and with pleasure in some form. In case you should happen to be a lazy Libran ("lovely" and "lazy" are two adjectives often used to describe people of your sign), you could experience many a frustration or confinement dream, for the simple reason that in your waking hours you are not really going after your desires and goals. If you are too indecisive too often, insecurity dreams may plague you, while too much self-indulgence in sense pleasures may produce the more unpleasant kind of sensuous dream. Once you learn to understand your dreams, to grasp the "messages" your subconscious is trying to get across to you, you then—having faced up to the matter—have the choice of taking specific measures to correct any unpleasant situation.

Your Special Abilities and Talents These are in the realm of your conscious, waking-hours state, and you are undoubtedly aware of many of your abilities and talents. You have an ability to maintain an objective viewpoint when other people are getting all heated up emotionally, and the capacity to be totally fair and impartial when judging another person and giving credit where it's due, even if you do not like the person. Sometimes this fine, objective, detached judgment of yours can be disappointing to your friends, for in trying to view a situation impartially, you might side against someone you really care for, though that individual would much prefer you to be biased in his behalf. You also have the ability to keep your temper, to remain calm, courteous, and cool headed in the midst of heated situations. On the rare occasions when you do lose your temper, everyone had better watch out, but that's a different story; invariably, you are the one who generates the aura of calm friendliness.

With regard to your talents, fashion design, interior design, and architecture are typically Libran professions. Being an air-sign person, you have a flair for communication, an ease of expression that can make you a fluent writer, speaker, teacher, salesperson, or advertising copywriter. Most pronounced, though, is your talent for design, for whether in fashion, home decor, or architecture, your unconscious urge is to balance and to relate. This, plus your Venus-based sense of beauty and harmony, enable you to blend form, color, and pattern most attractively. You may use this talent on your own home, wardrobe, and appearance, or in a professional way.

Your interest in cultural matters, too, may be accompanied by special talents in art, music, or writing, while in a more general way Librans are frequently successful as models, actors or actresses, receptionists, or in any career where they are on view and can utilize their attractive appearance and personal charm.

All of these abilities and talents can, of course,

either be used or neglected. Sometimes you tend to procrastinate, Libra, whether it's because you just can't make up your mind to get going, or whether it's that lazy streak we mentioned. This sort of thing is apt to show up in your dreams, when you experience situations or dream relationships which leave you with a distinct impression that there was a missing ingredient, or when you feel that in some way you failed to perform what was expected of you. If you appraise your recent past, you might find an occasion or two when you did indeed neglect to follow up on a promising opportunity, simply because you lacked the "go-ahead" spark at the moment. Even in a love relationship (in which, ordinarily, you excel!) there may have been someone to whom you unfortunately presented the more indolent side of your nature, sitting back and basking in the attention and pampering without really offering much in the way of interest or enthusiastic response. Or perhaps it was a job or social opportunity, which would have required a little exertion on your part or prompt action (you can be quite a latecomer when the lazy streak is upon you). It's true that when Librans are in top form (which means in good balance, with priorities in order), they are healthily opportunistic in their quick response to chances to get ahead. Negatively, when the scales are out of balance, you tend never quite to get around to doing what you intended to do. This sort of negativity produces many a "down" type of dream, through which your subconscious is trying to drum into your head the need to get on with it!

Both astrology and dreams are aids in realizing your full potential. And considering what your most important desires are—and what they cost in terms of both money and personal commitment—you should aim to utilize your full potential to achieve them.

How Do You Dream? Undoubtedly the surroundings in which you dream are graced with plumped pillows, elegant bed linens, and exotic coverlets, plus a pleasing view on which to feast your eyes as you awaken. Nothing will be out of place. You are worse than Virgo when it comes to order and neatness, sharing with that sign a dislike of loud noises, strident voices, and dissension in your environment.

The question, How do you dream? refers more to the content and meaning of your dreams than to physical setting or mood. Remembering dreams takes a bit of training and practice. Repeat nightly as you are falling asleep, "I will remember my dreams"; in time your efforts will pay off.

For the most part, your dreams will be peopled, colorful, and probably a bit scattered. Air-sign people tend to have a short attention span and this shows up in fragmented dream episodes. However, even the shortest most disconnected dream has a meaning, and your job is to relate it to real-life situations, past or current. Whatever the subject matter of your dream, the impression it leaves on you is important for it is often the clue to the meaning of the dream. The feeling left by a dream often mirrors an impression received in waking hours. For instance, you may have met someone socially who gave you the impression of being untruthful or evasive. You may subsequently have a dream in which you are searching for an object or are defending yourself against a verbal or physical onslaught, or are feeling uneasy about a dream event which, on the surface, seemed all right. Such a dream would relate to the real-life encounter, leaving you with the impression of uncertainty, suspicion, fear, or bafflement.

What Specific Dream Categories Mean to You

Confinement Dreams Except for the precognitive dream, in which the dream incidents are subsequently manifested in your waking hours, most dreams are not warnings that explicit events are about to engulf you. Therefore, do not become alarmed if you dream you are locked in a jail, house, barn, car, or warehouse! This is the confinement dream, the real meaning of which is that you yourself have cut off your escape route from some situation which you would dearly like to get out of. You may have made a firm commitment or promise, or perhaps have done something that ended a relationship, or have made an irrevocable business or financial decision—and now you have second thoughts. In other words, you are confined by a decision which is of your own making, and your reaction, as it shows up in your dream, is to feel boxed in, unable to get out of the situation. The dream in which your arms, legs, or voice seem to be paralyzed is also a confinement dream. Once you have recognized the source of your dilemma, waking-hours concentration on how to remedy the situation will make it unnecessary for your subconscious to dredge it up. If it cannot be remedied, at least you've got it into the light of day, faced up to it, and forced it out of the murky realm of your subconscious.

Insecurity Dreams This widespread type of dream represents, of course, some matter about which you subconsciously feel insecure, though the subject of the dream may have little to do with the subject you're insecure about. Loss, searching and not finding, missing travel connections, or nervously buzzing about in dream episodes with the definite sense of lacking some vital object or possession are all marks of the insecurity dream. The most prevalent of these include the loss of money and public appearance without enough clothes on. The missing clothes dream, whether it's part of your attire that's not there when you expect it to be or you standing stark naked in Macy's window, represents insecurity about your status or reputation—the fear that some peccadillo of yours will be exposed to public view. You Librans usually tend to have concern for your reputation, though you're not obsessive about it (and, subtle as you are, you invariably manage to keep any really sneaky things in your life well hidden), but a missing-clothes dream could be a subconscious fear that a secret of yours will be discovered. Probably the only message of that dream would be to have a convincing explanation ready, just in case! If you dream of a lost article or, in fact, if any dream episode makes you feel insecure, it could indicate either a personal or business/financial situation in which you are indeed insecure in your waking hours. It could be job security, whether or not you're going to receive expected funds, or a relationship that's begun to exhibit signs of shakiness. The point is that once you can identify, through your dream, the actual matter about which you feel insecure, you may be able to alleviate the causes of your insecurity; at least it will not haunt your dreams. You Librans may also experience insecurity dreams when you are deliberating a decision, considering various angles of a proposed course of action. While you're swaying there on the pendulum, unable as yet to determine on which side of the scale to balance the weight, that's when you could have your insecurity dreams.

Frustration Dreams These dreams differ from confinement and insecurity dreams because "outside forces" seem to frustrate your intentions. Someone isn't there when you expect him to be, or a party was canceled and you didn't know it, or wherever you are there is some sort of bafflement or confusion that frustrates you. Often you hear people say, "I dreamed I was in my house—only it wasn't at all like my house—and a stranger walked in . . ." This is an example of a frustration dream because the familiar becomes unfamiliar and the unexpected occurs, while the dreamer is unable to cope with it—a frustrating experience, which usually reflects subconscious self-doubts in the dreamer. In this type of dream, as in most dreams, you also have to realize that very often the person in your dream is a projection of yourself. A stranger walking into your house, for example, breaking things or otherwise behaving badly, could be a subconscious projection of your recent misbehavior in a friend's home; not that you necessarily broke things, but you could have been inconsiderate or discourteous, and now it's nagging at your subconscious a bit. Your frustration could stem from the delicacy of the situation. Maybe you flirted with your friend's husband or wife, and to apologize would be to emphasize it unwisely. So consider whether the individuals in your dreams are really themselves or projections of *you.* You see, subconsciously you want to spare yourself any blame or implication of wrongdoing, so your subconscious obliges in your dreams by focusing the guilt away from you!

Passive Dreams This is the sort of dream in which you figuratively sit back in your easy chair and watch the story unfold. You observe but you do not participate, even as you watch yourself "up there on the screen" moving about or speaking. Actually Librans are not especially prone to this type of dream, the purpose of which is to teach the dreamer to be objective, detached, and to view a specific situation impartially and comprehensively. Since you are naturally inclined to this sort of mental approach, there is not so much need for your subconscious to drive the point home. However, there may be an emotional involvement in your life that has caused you to go overboard a bit and abandon your objective outlook; this sort of dream could relate to your loss of perspective. During your waking hours, emotional bias would tend to obscure the overview, but in the dream you have stepped outside the scene and can observe all facets of the situation. Pay attention to the action and/or dialogue in the passive dream, as this will provide clues for fuller understanding of the real-life matter.

Action Dreams These dreams find you in motion, with a strong sense of vim, vigor, and sometimes urgency. You may be walking, running, climbing stairs, jogging, or jumping; or you might be on your way to a specific destination, perhaps carrying a suitcase or packages, and you can actually feel your steps on the pavement, the weight of the packages in your arms. In other words, this is the opposite of the passive dream, for in this dream episode you are a full participant in the action. And the action—whatever it may be—is decisive. As a Libran, you may experience the action dream whenever you need to be reminded that the time for deliberation is drawing to a close and the time for action is now. Your subconscious is nudging you to "fish or cut bait." Usually this sort of dream will refer to a matter that you've mulled over and reflected on for some time, and you may be just on the verge of making up your mind about it. If the action in the dream is unpleasant—if you are knocking yourself out running about or have the feeling of being on a treadmill, running like mad simply to stay in the same place—it could be that you dread taking specific action in a real-life matter. You Librans sometimes do tend to believe that if you don't do anything about a problem maybe it will go away! The action dream can be your subconscious reminding you that you can speed the departure of a problem by taking the initiative. The action dream is also a reminder that you have free will and can determine your own destiny. Relate the dream to a current situation in your life, in which you are likely to have to make a decision, choice, or commitment. Any suggestion of selection in your dream (even if it's something as simple as looking at a menu and deciding what to order) means that you are being faced with a choice, and your action dream is preparing you to be dynamic and decisive about it.

Recurring Dreams These are dreams that you have more than once. It may be a long time before the dream recurs, or perhaps you will dream it several nights in a row. In any case, this dream is an exact duplicate of the previous dream, or it is so similar in content, setting, and the impression it leaves with you, that you have a feeling of revisiting a particular scene and encountering the same people under similar conditions. This is always an important dream, for there is something in your subconscious that needs to be brought to light and attended to—whether it's a problem to be settled, a relationship matter that should be ironed out, or a particular quality, trait, or attitude of yours that needs modifying. Since you have repeated exposure to the recurring dream, you should be able to note and remember the details of it. In general, if there is a person (or persons) in your recurring dream, the matter in question is a relationship. Although the individual in your dream is not necessarily the individual involved in the real-life relationship, you can identify him or her by the actions and attitudes of the dream figure. For instance, your recurring dream may feature a childhood schoolmate with whom you never got along, but in the dream he or she is charming and lovable. This could relate to another person about whom you have ambiguous feelings, and the question may be whether or not to trust this person and accept him at face value. Here the impression left with you by the dream is important, for it may well be that you should accept this real-life person, but with reservations, and should be on the lookout for possible hidden motives. In other words, think about current situations in your life and analyze the recurring dream as it might relate to a specific matter.

Escape Dreams One of the nicest things about an escape dream is the fact that you wake up refreshed, energetic, ready to go! These dreams are comparatively rare and usually feature your joyful departure from an unpleasant situation and your happy arrival in a new environment or more exciting set of circumstances. In the escape dream you may elude pursuers and find safety, and you may close the door on work and drudgery and embark on an exhilarating adventure. You may fly off into the wild blue yonder (perhaps in a plane, perhaps by simply launching yourself off the ground and flying away; flying on one's own represents the ultimate in escape dreams). Freedom is the keynote of the escape dream and reflects your subconscious wish to rid yourself of a responsibility, burden, or other restrictions in your waking life. Sometimes your escape dream provides clues as to how you can lessen problems if not escape them entirely. The key may be an individual in your dream or (common in this sort of dream) a sudden surge of knowledge and sense of resolution that the action precipitating your dream escape is the absolutely right one to take. This insight, translated into practical, workable real-life expression, can be helpful. For the most part, though, escape dreams are really sort of mini vacations from the tensions and pressures of everyday living. They serve the purpose of releasing built-up tensions and put you in a good frame of mind to face the day's events, which in itself is a positive effect.

Sex Dreams There is usually no complicated message in the sex dream. It is a simple matter of your sex drive, which if not satisfactorily expressed in waking hours is diverted into dream expression. There is also the matter of how much of your waking time is devoted to sexual activity, sexual thoughts, preoccupation with sex in general. The more you concentrate on a subject during conscious waking hours, the less it will be featured in dreams—dreams being the outcropping of material tucked away in your subconscious. So if you are a really sexy Libran (which the majority of you are!), you'll undoubtedly be married or otherwise involved in sexual activity in real life, so there will not be the need for your subconscious to promote it in dreams. There are exceptions, of course, particularly if you have an unrecognized or unadmitted sexual attraction to someone, which is accordingly repressed and buried in your subconscious. In which case you may dream of having sex with that individual or someone who represents that person. It is a fascinating fact that one's partners in sex dreams are very rarely those individuals with whom one really desires to have sexual relations. The sex partner in a dream is usually "masked"—in terms of being the type, age, or general image of one to whom you are really attracted. Your subconscious sex desire for your friend's mate, for example, may produce a dream in which you are having sex with a relative, priest, nun—in other words, a taboo figure. The friend's mate is "off limits," so you dream of an equally off-limits type. Or your unacknowledged sexual attraction to your older boss may produce a dream in which you're having sex with someone older than you. You Librans are affectionate as well as sexy. If your real-life partner does not provide enough affection, you may experience modified sex dreams, in which there is a lot of foreplay but no real action.

Sensuous Dreams The sensuous dreams do not necessarily involve sex, but feature more often the senses of sight, hearing, smell, touch, and taste. In this type of dream you vividly experience these sensations, seeing colors with heightened perception, or hearing sounds with unusual clarity (particularly the timbre of an individual's voice). Or you may smell an identifiable perfume (even to the point of knowing the exact brand name), or taste a food in which you recognize all the little gourmet additions, or touch, stroke, squeeze, or hold an object that is as real to you as it could ever be in waking-hours. This kind of tactile dream experience, incidentally, represents evaluation; your subconscious is reminding you of a need to assess and weigh a certain matter—something that you as a Libran are naturally inclined to do anyway, but may have slipped up on in this particular case. When your sensuous dreams are unpleasant (hearing discordant sounds, smelling offensive odors, feeling sick from food you eat), the negative feelings you experience relate to some waking-hours overindulgence of one of your senses. If the dream is pleasant, it accents your feeling of appreciation for a recent waking-hours pleasure or a happy incident. If in your sensuous dream you are especially impressed by the exquisite beauty of what you experience through one of your senses, this is your subconscious awakening your creative urges, although your real-life expression of creative talent may not mirror the dream subject. Your dream of a richly hued oil painting or fabulously textured fabric, for instance, could be analagous to your coming up with a brilliantly creative business scheme.

Precognitive Dreams This is the dream that, subsequently, comes true. The real-life event may be an exact duplication of the dream event, or it may be that the general theme of the dream is reflected in an actual happening shortly afterward. You might, for example, dream that you get word of a friend's illness, while the subsequent event concerns business reverses of a relative (in both cases, the news was bad). Some people have frequent precognitive dreams; others merely think they do! Don't strain too hard to tie in actual events with your night-before dreams. The true precognitive dream is usually unmistakable, for there will be at least one definite link between dream and reality. The link may be news, travel, or a glimpse of the past (a common precognitive dream, where you dream of someone you haven't thought about in years and a few days later meet them on the street). Or the link may be the emotion engendered by the dream: elation, surprise, sadness, worry, and so on. More rare is the exact duplication between the dream and the following event. In waking hours Librans tend to be intuitive, so you could experience an occasional precognitive dream. If one of these dreams is extremely impressive, the sort of dream you cannot forget—and then it comes true—your subconscious could be showing you that you are more intuitive, more tuned in, than you may think.

Peopled Dreams Your dreams probably include quite a few people, mostly known to you. (Some individuals tend to dream of many strangers or faceless crowds.) Here, again, it is the relationship factor of Libra that is operative, and you would tend to have definite links with the people of whom you dream. No matter whether the setting is social, or you dream of people you work with, neighbors, family members, romantic companions, there would be a relationship of one sort or another between you and these others. However, the people of whom you dream may not necessarily represent their real-life counterparts; for instance, a dream of your father could be significant in terms of your relationship with your boss or teacher (the father representing the authority figure); or your dream of a former friend, with whom you had an argument and broke off the friendship in real life, could relate to a competitive situation currently existing in your waking hours (competition for a job, in love, in financial deals). The former friend would represent the adversary or competitor. Don't forget that you yourself may be projected in your dream as another individual—especially if that person is "guilty" of something and needs to be punished (your subconscious sparing you the accusation and making the other person the scapegoat!).

Symbols in Dreams As you will have noted, there is much symbolism in dreams. But occasionally you will have a dream in which a symbol is so emphatic that its significance is unmistakable. You may see a particular color, or a numeral (or someone's voice reiterating a number), or it may be an animal or an abstract design, or a mountain peak, or a rainbow. Such symbols tend to represent abstract qualities, such as aspiration (the mountain peak), optimism (the rainbow); or the color may relate to a specific event in your life (the powder blue was the color of your first party dress, or the shiny bronze was the color of your first car, and so on).

You may dream of one of the elements—fire, earth, air, water—which are also astrologically meaningful. Fire represents the spirit, earth the material body, air the mind, and water the emotions. The element of air is especially significant for you, as yours is an air sign. If you dream of flying—looking at stars, clouds, blue skies—or feel the wind or a soft breeze in your dream, this shows your potential for mental expansion and could mean a current opportunity to improve your mind or add to your knowledge. An unpleasant dream involving air (turbulent gusts of wind or hurricanes) shows that your thinking has taken a wrong turn somewhere. Air-related dreams and fire-related dreams are compatible with your temperament and signify that your subconscious is reminding you to fulfill your potential.

If you dream of an animal, your own feelings toward the animal will be what's important; if you fear animals or if they make you feel uneasy, dreaming of one will relate to similar reactions you're having toward a person currently in your life. On the other hand, if you like animals and have an affinity for certain species, to dream of one can mean a happy personal relationship in real life, or that some individual is arousing your love (not necessarily romantically). If you should dream of the number three, the color green, or of any item at all resembling a scale or other weighing instrument, that dream will have special meaning; your subconscious is focusing, through symbolism, on your need to find (and hold on to) your true identity, and possibly also giving you a clue as to your life mission.

Chapter 11

Scorpio

(October 24–November 22)

Your unconscious is the source of your natural instincts, while in your subconscious are found your innermost desires, some of which you may not even be aware. Your Sun sign represents the essential you: your individuality and uniqueness. Because you are a Scorpio, your dreams reflect this individuality, through which your unconscious and subconscious are expressed.

SCORPIO is a water sign, ruled by Pluto, fixed in quality (which means stable and steady). The combination of the water element and the fixity of your sign is apparent in your temperament, for you are emotion-oriented and fixed in your desires, opinions, and habits. You are the most intensely personal type in the Zodiac. Because of your deep emotional feelings, it is difficult for you to get an overview of a situation, objectivity is not your strong point. There is invariably a personal bias in your thinking, which can be favorable or unfavorable depending on the circumstances. You are exceedingly loyal to those you love, so would indeed be personally biased on their behalf. Conversely, you can be just as much *against* as you can be *for,* and in the case of persons you dislike, no amount of proof as to their good qualities would change your personal bias against them.

The association of Pluto with your sign adds a further complexity to your nature, for this is the planet of the underworld, and of the hidden, submerged depths in man. You are at your most Plutonian when you are secretly making plans, carefully refraining from revealing your motives, working behind the scenes on ideas and projects which come to light only when *fait accompli.* The subjects of your secrecy may be worthy or unworthy, but the method is the same in either case. Scorpio is known as the sign of extremes. Whatever you do, you do it wholeheartedly, which can lead to great "ups" or great "downs." Your ability to manage and direct people (often without their knowing it) equips you for an executive position, while your talent for delving into hidden areas can lead to a career in science, medicine, research, investigative work.

Your Unconscious Instincts You have strong urges to probe and to possess. You invariably seek to find the deeper meanings in any given situation, whether it's a question of looking behind the headlines to discover the real motives of public figures or the real causes of global events—or of probing to find out the explicit "why" of your mate's or friend's little white lie to you. You often mull over people's casual comments to determine what's really going on in their minds and what their intentions are. In other words, you are decidedly not a superficial type, nor do you accept anything at face value. All of which makes it well-nigh impossible to deceive you, for one way or another you will find out the truth! Your intuitive awareness lets you know when anything's going on that's the least bit sneaky. You can spot a phony, a liar, or a cheat at first glance. As a matter of fact, your first impressions of people are invariably one hundred percent accurate and you rarely have cause to change your mind about them. Although you yourself may be a totally honest, moral, high-principled person, you do have this sort of inborn awareness of evil and not only can spot it in others but instinctively know how to combat it.

Your urge to possess is manifested both tangibly and intangibly. In personal relationships this is expressed through your tendency to be possessive and somewhat jealous of the other person. You stand guard over what is yours, and no one had better try to take it away from you! Some of you Scorpios are extremely attached to material possessions, and though you can be generous to a fault with those you love, what is yours is yours and you do not part too easily with anything. In an intangible way, you like to possess facts, information, and especially secrets. Here, too, wild horses cannot drag a secret or confidential information from you, but you are extremely generous with advice, facts, and tips for those you care for.

These unconscious urges to probe and to possess are as natural to you as breathing and show up in many of your everyday actions and habits. They can, of course, be modified by other factors in your personality, and can be recognized, nurtured, and directed into positive expression by an act of the conscious will. These instincts are constantly operative, awake or asleep, and form a background to your dreams. However, the majority of your dreams are produced by . . .

Your Subconscious Desires Subconsciously, you wish for power and passion. That sounds quite dramatic—but Scorpio is a dramatic sign! However, these subconscious desires also show up in everyday situations. Your desire for power is often channeled toward professional ambition, whereby you aspire to be the president of a corporation, or to operate your own business or profession, or to achieve a managerial position in your current job. This does, in fact, give you a certain amount of power over others, though being a sensible and considerate Scorpio you do not try to dominate to any marked degree. As a matter of fact, yours is the more subtle way in any case. You operate through the power of suggestion, planting ideas in people's minds so that they quite willingly do what you want and often think it was their own idea to begin with! In effect, you can manipulate people and situations without appearing to do so. This, of course, can be good or bad, depending on your motives, but the technique would be the same.

Your desire for power is expressed on the domestic scene in much the same way, and lucky is the family who has a fine, loving Scorpio at the helm, for that family will ever be guided to its own best advantage. Although you can be extremely effective in direct confrontation, you prefer to use more subtle methods of getting people to agree with you. You accomplish this by pointing out the benefits they will gain by seeing things your way, and you instinctively know to which of their interests to appeal. If you are a "solid citizen" type who is interested in your home and community, yours can indeed be a powerful—though not strident—voice in community affairs. You also have a flair for financial dealings, and since money is one of the greatest sources of power in life, you usually aim to amass as much of it as you can.

Your desire for passion is not limited to sexual activity, though it must be admitted that since Scorpio is the sign that rules sex, you do have an extra perception of, and attraction to, sexual matters. However, in the broader context your desire for passion means that kind of singleminded dedication to a goal, an individual, a concept, an ideal. You are definitely not a halfway person nor a lukewarm person. You are an all-or-nothing person. As Scorpio is one of the (if not the) strongest signs in the

Zodiac in terms of character qualities, personal and physical magnetism, and force of will, it could well be said that everything you do, you do with passion. In creative expression, your work is strikingly dramatic, carrying a forceful message. In business or professional goals, you can work long hours, taking on projects that would ordinarily require several people to handle, and totally dedicate yourself to achieving a special objective. Passionate devotion to work, financial progress, creative expression, humanitarian aims, national or even global principles, are the hallmarks of Scorpio.

In your personal life, your desire for passion may be sexually oriented, or it may be in the realm of emotions. You are capable of deep and intense love, and can be loyal, faithful, passionate, in your devotion to the love of your heart. You also expect the same in return—and woe unto the individual who cheats on you! This is when those often-mentioned traits of vindictiveness and vengeance might come into play. For you can, we are sorry to say, be just as passionate in your desire to get even as you can be in other things, though if you are a positive, evolved Scorpio, you do control this tendency. Because you are hardly a wishy-washy person, you would not be apt to have wishy-washy dreams. In fact, your dreams tend to be involved and complex, with many a hidden meaning, as befits one whose natural instinct is to probe into secret ways. By being aware of both your unconscious instincts and your subconscious desires, you will be in a better position to interpret the meanings of your dreams.

Your Special Abilities and Talents These are in the realm of your waking hours, your conscious state, and you are no doubt aware of some of your special abilities and talents. Important among these is your ability to be patient which—in a way—is surprising in one of your strong, dynamic temperament. But you do have patience when you can see that, ultimately, your goals will be accomplished. You can wait while assiduously working; and the waiting does not at all dim your keen enjoyment of achievement when it does come. You also have the ability to be exceptionally self-disciplined; in fact, self-discipline is a must for you Scorpios—a fact that you usually learn early in life and perhaps somewhat painfully. Like Aries, you tend to welcome challenges, and derive a special kind of satisfaction from overcoming obstacles. Almost anything in life that's worth doing or achieving does demand a certain amount of self-discipline, and this sort of price you are perfectly willing to pay.

Your ability to remember, and to learn from experience, is another plus. Some people tend to make the same mistakes over and over again. Not you Scorpios. Once burned, twice shy, is certainly true of you, and whether this applies to actions or habits which resulted in unpleasant experiences, or to an individual who fooled you once but will never fool you again, you store your experiences in your capacious memory bank, where they are ever ready for reference. This is also the case when you have some sort of score to settle. Here, too, you can wait forever, but sooner or later you know you will get your chance to pay off the debt. Actually, harboring grudges, though rather a typical Scorpio tendency, is negative and will show up in your dreams unpleasantly. It is far healthier to forgive grievances, even if you do not forget them (which is unlikely anyway!). But any in-turning negativity does sometimes wreak havoc in your subconscious, perhaps subjecting you to dreams in which you are harassed, persecuted, pursued—and especially to the confinement dream, where you are indeed boxed in by your own negative thought patterns.

One of your greatest strengths is the ability to

totally change your own life. Scorpio is the sign of regeneration, of spiritual rebirth, and very often a Scorpio person who has all the faults in the book and who is living a completely negative, harmful, or depraved life style, will do an about-face and become the polar opposite of what he once was. This takes guts, a powerful will, self-discipline, and determination, all of which you Scorpios have in abundance.

With regard to your talents, business, government, and the humanitarian fields of medicine, education, or social service often appeal to Scorpio people. You like to feel that what you do really matters, and while many of you direct this urge toward personal relationships (raising a good family in a fine healthy environment certainly matters, perhaps most of all), others among you seem to be called to careers which benefit many. Scientific research, psychiatry, and psychology are also Scorpio fields, while on a more down-to-earth level, personnel work, any form of counseling, or jobs where you listen to people's problems and complaints, and direct them accordingly, would fit your temperament and talents. That detective-like streak in your nature actually makes Scorpio people excellent at investigative work, while along business lines, insurance, health and hospital programs, or investment counseling are among the fields in which you could successfully work. Because Scorpio also relates to death (the mystical connection of death, spiritual rebirth, regeneration) jobs in funeral parlors, cemeteries, or crematoriums are also possibilities.

Your excellent memory, an ability to organize and to direct others, a talent for research, and a flair for financial dealings equip you for many and varied occupations. But all of your abilities and talents can, of course, be either utilized or neglected. Mostly it depends on your motivation, for as a

Scorpio, the motive is the real power. Achieving the goal is easily done, with your attributes. Your dreams will certainly reveal to you whether you are making the most of your abilities and talents or whether you are neglecting them. If the latter, your nights are apt to abound with frustration dreams, confinement dreams, insecurity dreams, as your subconscious labors mightily to prod you into positive action. Since the aftermath of such dreams includes awakening with feelings of depression, discontent, sluggishness, and/or resentment, this becomes a vicious circle, for you are hardly put in the mood to go out and conquer the world! By identifying the reasons behind your frustrations or insecurities, you bring them into the light of consciousness, where they are easier to handle—and are able to do something to remedy the situation, in true turnabout Scorpio fashion.

How Do You Dream? In the first place, you are probably a deep sleeper, who goes hurtling off into dreamland with the same intensity you show in many other activities. But just in case you are an insomniac, or a fitful sleeper, and provided there is no physical or health reason for this, your wakeful condition stems just as much from your subconscious as do your dreams. You could be reluctant to face whatever it is that's on the dream agenda for the night. Even if you do not remember your dreams—perhaps especially if you do not remember them—it's still your subconscious, blotting out in one way or another, your confrontation with that inner self of yours in dreams. Of course, you may be a Scorpio who sleeps peacefully and dreams pleasant dreams, but just in case you belong to the wakeful category, interpreting your dreams can be most helpful in zeroing in on the cause of your slumber problems. With your self-discipline, you should be easily able to train your mind to recall dream episodes upon awakening. Once you do have this faculty well in hand, you will probably find that your dreams are less disconnected than the dreams of most people. You are more inclined to produce complete episodes, and whether or not the dream events appear to have significance, they undoubtedly do. You would also tend to have symbolic dreams, sensuous dreams, possibly sex dreams. Because you Scorpio people have a full and healthy awareness of sex during most of your waking hours (this does not become a preoccupation unless you allow it to do so—your awareness is simply a part of the total you), you would not experience sex dreams all that frequently. Your dreams may often include color (the average dream is in black and white or off-gray), which signifies creative power. Many of you have precognitive dreams, tuned in as you are to spiritual forces and occult phenomena.

What Specific Dream Categories Mean to You

Confinement Dreams Any dream in which you are closed into some place or area, and cannot get out, is a confinement dream. The whole focus of the dream is on your attempting to escape and being unable to do so. Sometimes there is specific danger in the dream, which you know is coming your way and you frantically try to escape before it strikes; or, it may be a vague sense of impending doom from which you are attempting to flee. Confinement dreams may be very explicit (you are tied up, or locked in, or in some sort of "trap"). Or the sense of confinement in the dream may be along mental lines; you somehow "know" that you are caught or otherwise totally restricted. In the first place, this sort of dream is completely symbolic. Even if your dream should be very extreme (and being a Scorpio, it could be), such as finding yourself imprisoned and about to be executed, you need not fear that this is a forerunner of some tragedy. The confinement dream always means that something you have said or done—or something that you have not said or done when you should have—has put you into an unpleasant situation. Remorse may play a part in the confinement dream, too. You yourself have created a situation in which you feel boxed in, and until you take steps in your waking hours to remedy the matter, you could be subject to this type of dream. You may, for example, have neglected to do a good deed for a friend who counted on you, when you really could have done so. As a result, the friendship could have been undermined, and as it was actually your fault, your confinement dream represents you trapped in the unhappiness of the broken friendship. Or, perhaps in one of your darker Scorpio moods you punished another individual too severely for some transgression—you made the punishment worse than the crime. There might be a bit of remorse here, combined with an attitude of self-justification; but your subconscious is reminding you that in punishing another, you are punishing yourself, too—confined in a net of your own making.

Insecurity Dreams We all experience insecurity dreams from time to time, as they stem from anxiety and from a real-life situation about which we feel insecure, and there are certainly plenty of those. In this dream, loss, lack, and search are the keynotes. It may be your purse or wallet or some other valued object that's suddenly missing; or you may lack something in your dream that you certainly expected to have (like your clothes); or you are frantically searching for something important to you—a lost briefcase, a missing child, a strayed pet, or a stolen car. Anxiety and nervousness dominate this dream, which invariably reflects a waking-hours situation about which you are anxious and nervous. You might be concerned that the reshuffling of personnel in your office will result in your being given an unwanted assignment or being dismissed. Your dream of a lost wallet would indeed represent a threat to your security that you are experiencing in real life. Or your love affair may be steadily deteriorating, and your dream of searching for a missing child or pet could represent your subconscious quest to restore the love (the child or pet symbolizing the love object). If you can relate your insecurity dream to the waking-hours situation about which you are insecure, at least this will enable you to identify the cause of the dream instead of compounding your problems by awakening with anxiety and bafflement and not knowing why. Also, once a problem is viewed in the light of day, faced up to, and dealt with in practical, objective terms, you are less likely to experience this particular type of dream.

Frustration Dreams In the frustration dream, you are prevented from achieving a specific objective. This may be because you wake up or because the dream scene shifts in one of those inexplicable ways that dreams have, and suddenly you're somewhere else, with the nagging feeling that an incompleted act was terribly important but you can't quite place what it was. Or in your dream some "outside force" prevented you from accomplishing your objective. (The door was closed and locked when you got there, or the train or plane had left when you arrived at the terminal, or the person you were rushing to meet never showed up.) In any case, it's never your fault that the dream act was not completed —which further adds to your sense of frustration. This sort of dream represents a real-life situation in which, at least for the moment, you feel powerless to act. For example, your job may be utterly miserable, but because you have a family to support you cannot simply walk out. Or your residence is too small, but you can't afford a larger place. Or you're in love with someone who is not free, or who does not reciprocate your feelings. Unless or until you find a way out of the real-life frustration dilemma, you may experience frustration dreams—though as often as not the dream itself appears to have no connection with the real-life matter.

It is the frustration that's the link between the dream and the reality. Sometimes you may not be aware of what is really frustrating you in your waking hours, as the problem may be more complex than the examples given. Your frustration dream provides clues to the source. The individual in your dream may represent a person who is the basic reason for your frustration (boss, family member, a certain associate), or the dream situation helps you to zero in on a real-life condition that's "eating away" at your subconscious via the frustration syndrome. By recognizing the source of your frustration, you can be motivated to doing something about it—if not immediately, then by better long-range planning of your future. As soon as decisive action is taken or contemplated, there will be no need for your subconscious to produce frustration dreams.

Passive Dreams This can be a valuable dream for you, as it accents the need for objective thinking—something you Scorpios sometimes find difficult to practice. In the passive dream, you are the watcher, not the participant. You view, as on a screen, the dream plot unfolding, observing yourself as well as others acting out whatever the dream plot may be, but experiencing no particular emotion or reaction. Inasmuch as Scorpio individuals tend to become very personally involved with other people and with situations, they are frequently biased or prejudiced in some way. Admit it! If your very best friend or lover becomes embroiled in an argument with someone else, you are decisively in his or her corner, regardless of whether or not your friend or lover may be wrong. This is not objectivity (though it's very nice for the friend or lover). The reverse can also be true. That neighbor who did you dirt in some way may have earned a particular honor or award, but you are not about to rejoice with him or her. In other words, your real-life emotional involvement in many and sundry matters does preclude detachment and objectivity, but your subconscious—recognizing the need for this—provides you with a passive dream now and then so that you may get the overview and see the dream episode more comprehensively. By relating your passive dream to a real-life situation or relationship, you can recognize the specific matter in which you need to step aside from your personal feelings and get the "big picture."

Action Dreams In these dreams, instead of the vague, shadowy, unreal sort of action often experienced in dreams (the slow run, the literally dreamlike quality of your physical motions), you have a sharp, keen awareness of your body moving. If you're walking you feel the ground beneath your feet, or you feel the objects that you grasp, or the motion and vibration of the car that you drive. Usually, there is some element of speed in the action dream. You are dashing along toward something—or away from something (if away from something, and you are anxious about it, then there is an element of the insecurity dream in this as well). The typical action dream, however, finds you expressing physically the quality of decisiveness. You're running up the stairs or down the street to an objective. Or, your dream activity is even more specifically decisive: buying tickets, signing documents, making unequivocal statements, and so on. The meaning of the action dream is that in your waking hours you have taken or are about to take a definite course of action about something. You make a decision to get married, or to break off an unrewarding relationship; to change jobs or start your own business; to begin a self-improvement program or join a health club. Your decision to act makes you feel good and your dream reflects this sense of accomplishment. If the action dream is unpleasant, then you should give further thought to a real-life decisive step you are contemplating. There would be some angle to it that might have unpleasant repercussions.

Recurring Dreams Sometimes the recurring dream pops up only two or three times in your whole life, or it can come more frequently. This dream may, each time, be an exact repeat as to detail, or it may be so similar in content, theme, and the impression it leaves with you, that it generates a sense of déjà-vu. Recurring dreams are always important, as your subconscious is drumming home a point of some sort which you refuse to recognize. If there are people in your recurring dreams, try to identify them as symbols or "images" of individuals in your current waking hours, remembering that a person in your dream may represent someone else. (A woman may represent the "mother" figure, your father can be an "authority" figure; often the child in your dream is you.) The subject matter of recurring dreams varies considerably, of course, among dreamers. It is the fact of recurrence that's important. So study this dream well if you experience it (some people never do) and connect it with a situation in your life or an attitude, habit, or fear of yours, for the recurring dream always carries a lesson.

Escape Dreams Usually the escape dream is a joy to experience, for in it you are freeing yourself from a restriction or burden. This may be expressed by your literally leaving the ground and flying off (all on your own; no plane!), and that is the purest form of the escape dream. Or you may leave behind your worries and cares, bad weather, or some other symbolic gloom, to find yourself in an indefinite sort of place where happiness, freedom, and sunshine abound. The reason for the escape dream is simple. You subconsciously wish to get away from responsibilities, work, burdens, a health problem, or emotional trauma. People generally don't have too many of these dreams, but after experiencing one of them you certainly awaken feeling great, ready to deal with the day's problems. In a way these dreams have therapeutic value, for they represent your subconscious relieving the pressure a bit, as well as gratifying your deep-seated wish for freedom.

Sex Dreams One would think that a Scorpio would have plenty of sex dreams, inasmuch as your sign rules sex and you're always being described as being the supersexy one of the Zodiac! However, Scorpio people experience sex dreams in just about the same proportion as do people of other signs—the determining factor being that the more satisfying your waking-hours sex life is, the less you will dream about this subject, and vice versa. The sex drive is one of the most powerful of instincts, and if it is unfulfilled in real life, your subconscious will attempt to fulfill it via dreams. It is interesting, though, that you Scorpios have such a keen *awareness* of sex (regardless of how active your sex life actually may be) that you tend to attribute sexual meanings and symbolism to many of your dreams that may not actually concern sex. In your waking hours, too, you are quicker than most to spot a hidden sexual meaning in anything (advertising, music, other people's comments). At any rate, your sex dreams may represent a release of sexual tensions or reveal to you a subconscious sexual attraction to an actual person, even though the partner of your sex dream may not be the same individual. In fact, dream sex partners are seldom those you wish they were; more likely they are symbols or images of someone with whom you would really like to have sex. There is also the fact that very often the subconscious recognizes the sex drive for what it is—merely a drive—and provides in the dream a partner (one might say that any partner will do) without surrounding the act with love, romance, or other emotional consideration.

Sensuous Dreams The sensuous dream is not necessarily related to sex, but focuses on the senses of sight, hearing, taste, touch, and smell. In this dream, one of the senses is particularly acute. The dreamer views vivid color, or hears impressive sound, smells an identifiable perfume or other scent, tastes specific food, or touches objects or material that feel every bit as real as their real-life counterparts. You Scorpios would probably tend to dream of the sense of touch more than of the other senses, for you are noted as being "touchers"—inclined to pat, squeeze, stroke, or otherwise use tactile perception. The meaning of your sensuous dream has to do with real-life indulgence of, or inhibition of, one of the senses. If you are dieting, for example, you might dream of eating delectable food, though, conversely, you might also dream that the food you are eating is making you sick. In either case, your subconscious is (a) gratifying your desire for food, or (b) reminding you that your overindulgence is making you fat or ill. In general, if your sensuous dream is unpleasant, it is a clue that you are, in your waking hours, overindulging one of your senses (though not necessarily the one in your dream). If it is a pleasant dream, it represents your savoring a recent or soon-to-be achieved triumph or pleasure. Or it could merely be a dream expression of your appreciation of life, vitality, good health, or personal satisfactions.

Precognitive Dreams You Scorpios are so tuned in to the upper planes of existence that even in your waking hours you may frequently experience precognition, having a "feeling" or a special awareness that something is going to happen and it does. Usually, people who utilize this gift in their waking hours have fewer precognitive dreams than those who block out such extrasensory perceptions. However, there are exceptions, and Scorpios could be among them, experiencing both real-life and dream precognitions. In this sort of dream, the subsequent real-life event is sometimes an exact duplication of the dream. You dream that you are walking down Main Street and you encounter your fifth-grade teacher, whom you haven't seen for years, and she is wearing blue. Two or three days later you meet her on Main Street and she is wearing blue. This sort of dream has no real significance in terms of the actual event, but serves rather as a subconscious reminder that you could well develop and encourage your intuitive faculty, your spiritual awareness, or maybe your creativity. Another type of precognitive dream comes true in essence if not in detail. You dream that your brother phones you with good news, and shortly afterward your husband comes home and beamingly announces he's got a raise. Good news in both cases. In case you are one of those Scorpios who has very meaningful precognitive dreams that always, or nearly always, give you a preview of actual events, you are undoubtedly in tune with the cosmic flow and need no interpretive advice from us!

Peopled Dreams You would tend to dream of people since your temperament is very much oriented toward involvement with others on a personal and emotional level. Remember that the people in your dreams are not always whom they seem to be—again, look for the image or the person represented by the dream individual if, when taken at face value, the dream seems to have no meaning. Keep in mind, too, that a person in your dream is frequently a projection of *you*. The dream individual with whom you are sympathizing because his or her love life has gone awry may be you indulging in a little subconscious self-pity because your own love life is unhappy or nonexistent. Or an individual who has acted badly in some way and is being rightfully punished could be you not consciously facing up to your peccadillo, but subconsciously feeling the need for chastisement anyway. If a dream person is not behaving in character, then he or she probably represents some other character in your life, or yourself. A straitlaced co-worker showing up in your dream drunk and disorderly may represent your Uncle John, who is noted for taking an extra few for the road (or maybe yourself at a recent event where you subconsciously fear you may have disgraced yourself). Look for correlations and analogies in your peopled dreams, if the person and his/her behavior do not seem to have meaning.

Symbols in Dreams Scorpios are prone to these phenomena, for while many a dream is loaded with symbolism of one kind or another, sometimes there are dreams in which a certain object or pattern will be especially impressive. It may be a certain color, or an animal, or a number, or an abstract design, or one of the elements (fire, earth, air, water). Astrologically, the elements are significant, for fire represents the spirit; earth, the material body; air, the mind; and water, the emotions. The element of water is especially meaningful for you, since yours is a water sign. To dream of a sea, a lake, a pond, a swimming pool, or rain relates to your current emotional state. If the water is calm, pleasant, enjoyable, then you are emotionally well balanced and in control. If the water is turbulent, it reflects emotional turmoil. A flood or other catastrophic watery dream signifies that you are in the process of being engulfed by your emotions and should strive for more objectivity. Earth-related dreams and water-related dreams are compatible with your temperament and can show that your subconscious is urging you to develop your full potential (in terms of your talent, or as a human being). Dreaming of an animal is symbolic only as the dream relates to your feelings about the animal. If you are fond of dogs, cats, turtles, or whatever, dreaming of one may feature this symbol as a love object. If you dislike animals, dreaming of one could denote a mistrust or fear of a certain individual in real life. If you should dream of the number nine, the colors red or brown, or of a scorpion, serpent, or eagle (yours is the only sign that has *three* symbols!), that dream will be significant. Your subconscious is focusing, through symbolism, on your true identity, possibly even on your basic mission in life . . . so, in true Scorpio fashion, delve into the mystic meaning of the symbolism.

Chapter 12

Sagittarius

(November 23–December 21)

Your natural instincts stem from your unconscious, while your subconscious is the realm of your deepest, innermost desires, some of which you may not consciously recognize. Your Sun sign represents your individuality, the essential you through which you express your instincts and desires. Because you are a Sagittarian, the contents and meanings of your dreams reflect your own unique individuality.

SAGITTARIUS is a fire sign, ruled by Jupiter, mutable in quality (which means flexible, adaptable). The blend of mutability and the fire element is shown in your temperament, for you are physically and mentally active, love nothing better than a mobile existence in which you do a lot of traveling, locally or distantly (as opposed to sitting day after day in one place). You also tend to make the best of any situation in which you find yourself, for Jupiter's association with your sign inclines you to be optimistic as well as philosophic. From Jupiter, too, stems your generally upbeat personality: your cheerfulness, openhandedness, generosity of spirit. The fire element corresponds with idealism and aspiration. Add to this the contagious enthusiasm which is a marked trait of yours, and it's no wonder that you have that special flair for inspiring others to follow along with you on your travels through life.

At the same time, although Jupiter has given you a tremendous gift—the ability to make friends—you are also highly independent and cherish your personal freedom. A wide circle of friends and a lot of lighthearted romance can make you very happy, especially when combined with an active on-the-go life style. You shy away from binding ties (which is why Sagittarians are known as the bachelors of the Zodiac—whether they be Mr. or Ms.). Of course Sagittarians *do* marry or get otherwise involved in meaningful relationships, but they are happiest in these arrangements when the bonds are not too restrictive. There's nothing devious in your makeup. In fact, your honest outspokenness can sometimes lead to a few problems. Since your motives are invariably without malice, though, no one stays mad at you for very long! You're a breezy, cheerful, fun-loving person, at your very best in a career or life style that takes you traveling and in which you can utilize your keen mind and idealistic principles.

Your Unconscious Instincts You have strong urges to aspire and to expand. Put in more down-to-earth terms, this means that your unconscious instincts orient you toward achievement, faith, hope, and noble principles. You are also compelled to widen your scope of knowledge, enlarge your circle of friends, and increase your material assets. It is said of Sagittarius that the young men see visions and the old men dream dreams. Equally applicable to females, of course, this points up your faith in the future. While you may be discouraged or depressed once in a while, as most people are, your natural bent is toward optimism. Despair is an unknown state to you. You often "feel lucky" and you often *are* lucky. The reference here is not necessarily to the track or gaming tables (though gambling, too, is a Sagittarian realm), but to your often being in the right place at the right time and "lucking into" a good job, or a travel opportunity, or an exciting new romance, or a nice bit of cash.

With your dynamic and irresistibly friendly spirit, it's no wonder that you can arouse enthusiasm in others, especially for an ideal or a principle. For this reason, Sagittarians make excellent teachers. They plant the seeds of aspiration in the young, who tend later to bear the fruit of such seeds. In a more simplistic way, though of equal importance, is the manner in which other lives are affected when ignited by your unique spark. Unintentionally, perhaps even casually, you can, with your cheerful ways, brighten the day for individuals who may be down in the dumps, discouraged, or hopeless. You give them an uplift, figuratively raise their eyes from contemplation of the dust to view the stars and what lies even beyond. Through you, others also aspire in the upward direction of hope.

Your urge to expand is expressed through a certain lavishness in your nature. Nothing petty or restricted for you, whether it's buying six fillets when you need only two, ordering a few dozen roses when six will make the centerpiece, or showering your loved ones with gifts and attention. An image of Sagittarius at its most typical is the picture of Jove (another name for Jupiter, your ruling planet) seated at the head of the festive table, with the horn of plenty spilling lavishly down the board and everyone eating, drinking, and making very merry! This is the principle of expansion at its most fruitful.

These unconscious instincts of yours reflect in many of your actions and habits. Unconscious instincts can be recognized, nurtured, directed into positive expression, and when necessary redirected. These instincts are constantly operative, whether you are asleep or awake, forming a backdrop to your dreams. However, the majority of your dreams are produced by . . .

Your Subconscious Desires Subconsciously, you desire freedom and mobility, which—to point out two typically Sagittarian proclivities—is why you are so attracted to travel and so reluctant to wed! Your desire for action produces in you a definite love of motion. Whether it's simply walking (you Sagittarians are great striders) or country hiking, skiing, swimming, or flying, you revel in being in motion. You Sagittarians frequently like sports, and when you do it's more likely to be a moving or "legs" sport, as opposed to games that are played in a restricted area. Cross-country skiing is your cup of tea, as well as long-distance marathons, sports-car racing, hiking the Appalachian Trail, and so on. In travel, you love the trip to a destination as much as or even more than the destination itself. It's the getting there, not the arrival, that you relish.

This same desire for mobility suits you for a job or career in which you can move about (the original traveling salesman must have been a Sagittarian!). You are not especially domestic and prefer to be out and about rather than spend quiet evenings at home. When you do stay home, you love to entertain hosts of friends and acquaintances, preferably on an informal basis.

Your desire for freedom shows up in your careful avoidance of situations that call for total commitment—whether in job or career, the family, or personal relationships. Some Sagittarians do not even like to sign leases, as this implies restriction should they wish to change residence before the lease is up. This urge for freedom makes for some complications in personal relationships at times. Though you Sagittarians are certainly romance-minded, you automatically look around for the nearest exit when it appears that a relationship is about to become binding. As a matter of fact, once you do get married or otherwise involved in a total-commitment situation—and provided your partner is neither possessive nor jealous—you are excellent mates, happy "in harness" and finding that it's not as bad as you thought it would be. You do need a loose rein, though. (Anyone interested in capturing the heart—and the commitment—of a Sagittarian would do well to use reverse psychology. Give him or her all the freedom in the world, and your Sagittarian will come prancing into the corral.)

Aside from matters of the heart, career, residence, and the like, your desire for freedom is also manifested in your mental attitudes and your interests. You are a nonconformist, not about to follow established traditions and customs unless you happen to believe in them, and enjoy off-beat hobbies and occupations. Just because a thing is "in" is no guarantee that it will be of interest to you.

With subconscious desires for freedom and mobility, your dreams should be most interesting, while a real nightmare to you would be the confinement dream! But since not every Sagittarian can live a life ideal for his temperament, you probably encounter many a minor frustration, insecurity, or confinement as you go along your way. Because you are adaptable and try to make the best of life as you find it, these frustrations will creep into your subconscious and manifest themselves in your dreams from time to time. Since you are extremely intuitive, probably more so than you realize, you may often awaken with the solution to a problem or the answer to a question, right there, fresh in your mind. In other words, your dreams—whether or not you remember them—not only provide you with clues concerning your dilemma, but even within the dream you quickly grasp the meaning and translate it into waking knowledge. As Sagittarius is the sign of prophecy, you are really tuned in to the upper planes, and this shows up in your dreams as well as in your waking hours. Interestingly enough, you are very casual about this, making no big deal when your "prophetic" and usually quite offhand comments are later proved to have indeed stemmed from a glimpse into the future.

Your Special Abilities and Talents Along with Gemini, yours is a sign of great versatility. Since your special abilities and talents are undoubtedly put to good use during your waking hours (or should be) you must be aware of many of them, such as your ability to make and maintain friendships, which not only has social benefits but works to your advantage in career matters as well. Or it could be your ability to take the broad, philosophic view when petty incidents and myriad minor details threaten to swamp you or those around you. You're a great one for taking a short break from everyday pressures for a bit of discussion about some abstract subject, after which everyone returns to the workbench refreshed. You have the ability to see the humor in life, even when the joke is on you (not everyone's humor extends that far!). And you have the ability to create a general feeling of good cheer, even when the situation or air around you is fraught with antagonisms. Your "get happy, I'm here" approach is effective more often than not. Then, too, your ability to be magnanimous in the face of defeat or someone else's vindictiveness has a truly noble touch about it. Although you can have a blazing temper at times (after all, yours is a fire sign) and you can, unfortunately, be impatient, brusque, or sarcastic on occasion, you are simply above anything suggestive of a planned retaliation or a coldblooded vendetta.

Your talents could be many, for you have a quick mind to learn new procedures, methods, work routines, and you pick up so many odd bits and pieces of knowledge along life's path that you have a regular storehouse of skills at your command. On the other hand, you may not always use your talents to best advantage, for their development requires dedicated study, practice, and self-discipline, and with your freedom-and-mobility orientation, you may have evaded that sort of thing. The result could be that you coast along in undemanding jobs or impermanent career situations. Superficiality is a danger for you as well as for Gemini, for although skimming along life's surface may be a pleasant way to proceed, when you're not fulfilling your real potential, you experience a nagging feeling of unease and discontent. Hastily pushed into the back of your subconscious, this shows up in your dreams.

Professions in which Sagittarians excel include teaching, writing, law, the ministry, publishing, and, of course, anything connected with the travel field. The communications media is a "natural" for you, as well as selling, advertising copywriting, acting, tutoring, sports, and anything at all to do with speculation (stocks and bonds, the investment field in general, and the entire galaxy of gambling-related activities).

All of your abilities and talents can, of course, be either utilized or neglected. With you, Sagittarius, it is more likely to be a case of sins of omission rather than commission when it comes to fulfilling your potential. While some people might misuse a talent, directing it to unworthy, even evil, ends, you are more apt to let a talent lie dormant as you carefully skirt any situation or life style that might require you to give your utmost. This tendency ties in with that general, noncommittal attitude of yours. But if you do have a specific talent, and particularly if it could be used to benefit many (such as teaching or writing), you are intuitively aware of the fact that you're slacking off where you should be buckling down; and your dreams will reaffirm this. Think about your life up to this point and see if there have been really good opportunities that you've sidestepped. Your friends often wish to be helpful and put opportunities in your path (this is indeed reciprocal, for you are an exceedingly helpful, generous-hearted person yourself), but did you follow up on that chance for an upper-echelon job, or did it seem to carry with it too much responsibility? Or what about that advanced-study course that would have cut into your freewheeling evenings on the town? Or remember that wonderful friend who became much more than a friend, but you backed away when you heard that echo of wedding bells?

Of course there's nothing that says you *must* tie yourself up in binding situations, but on the other hand, are you the type of Sagittarian who wants to be Peter Pan all your life? Your subconscious may be loaded with odds and ends of bypassed opportunity or unrealized talents, and if it is, you'll certainly hear about it in your dreams!

How Do You Dream? You are likely to dream in all sorts of environments (on planes, trains, buses, catnaps in your easy chair when TV gets boring), but it is the content and meanings of your dreams on which this question is focused. You Sagittarians tend to have far-ranging dreams, with many subjects, events, and people crowded into one night's excursions into dreamland. Reflecting your temperament, your dreams would be on the active side. You frequently experience a sense of urgency, of bustling about and rushing here and there for various but specific purposes. The typical Sagittarian dream is an extroverted one, often featuring extravaganzas in which you are an active participant: circuses, theatrical performances, parades, and so on tend to give an upbeat (though sometimes exhausting) theme to your dreams. Of course, like anyone else, you do have your quiet little dreams as well as the vague ones. In general, though, you are inclined to have multiple dream episodes, with each one being reasonably self-contained, often with a beginning, middle, and end, which is fairly unusual. A Sagittarian relating his or her dream almost always includes the expression " . . . and suddenly I found myself in the midst of all these people . . ." (or in Paris, at the seashore, on a mountaintop, wherever). You also tend to dream frequently in brilliant color rather than the usual black and white or muted hues of the average dream. Precognitive dreams and symbols in dreams, too, have high incidence on Sagittarian dream lists.

What Specific Dream Categories Mean to You

Confinement Dreams What a ghastly experience is your confinement dream! More in the nature of a nightmare. Since consciously, subconsciously, and unconsciously, your orientation is toward freedom, the confinement dream—in which you are closed in or boxed into someplace from which you can't escape—would certainly be upsetting and find you awakening with the jitters, to say the least. This sort of dream will always reflect a subconscious, current fear of yours that you have gotten yourself or are about to get yourself into a confining situation, which may be related to work, your residence, a relationship, or a long-term study course. But there is also another angle to the confinement dream, which is that the confinement is self-imposed, and whether it applies to one of the specific matters named above or to a more intangible situation, you're the one who got yourself into this mess! You may have hurt someone by your sharp, impatient words, and the fact that you didn't *intend* to hurt did not assuage the wounded feelings of the other person. So there you are with a damaged friendship on your hands and, for a Sagittarian, this is no small thing. Although your dream may feature you in a locked room or a prison cell, this doesn't mean you're about to get arrested. The real imprisonment has resulted from your own behavior, and will be present until you make amends or otherwise resolve the matter satisfactorily.

Insecurity Dreams Experienced by everyone, the insecurity dream accents the losing of something vital, the searching for something vital, and the general feeling of anxiety that you are lacking something that you should have. Very often the insecurity dream finds you suddenly without any money (your purse or wallet having inexplicably disappeared) or without all or part of your clothing in a public situation where by rights you should be fully dressed. This latter type of insecurity dream, in which partial or total public nudity is featured, is the acting out of your subconscious fear that something you would prefer to keep hidden has been or is about to be exposed. It could be a flirtation with your best friend's mate, hanky-panky on your income tax, or a sharp business maneuver which would not do your reputation any good if it was revealed. Mostly, though, the lost article (be it money, a possession, a pet, or another individual) represents your subconscious anxiety about a material matter—job, finances, property—or a relationship. The specific item in the dream may not be the same item you are insecure about in waking hours, though lost funds usually do tie in with material insecurity. Your impression upon awakening that you've certainly had an anxiety-filled night is the hallmark of the insecurity dream. If you have not faced up to a real-life situation as the source of your insecurity, your dream can help you to pinpoint it—after which down-to-earth practical strategies could help to resolve the matter, and your insecurity dreams would fade away. Until the next time, that is, for this is the most widely experienced type of dream.

Frustration Dreams These are dreams where you

cannot finish what you start, whether it's a trip, a meeting with someone, a sexual encounter, or some vital information you wish to impart or receive. And it's never your fault (in the dream, that is). Another individual isn't there when you expect him to be, or the place you're headed for turns out to be closed, or the dream scene changes just as you are about to do or say something of utmost importance, or you wake up—left with a feeling of frustration. This sort of dream can be very helpful in pointing up the real cause of a waking-hours frustration, a cause of which you are unaware or from which you've carefully averted your gaze. For instance, you might feel that if you didn't have so many bills to pay you could sign up for higher education or take a trip or look for a better job. Aside from the fact that you yourself may have run up the bills in the first place, or have a rightful responsibility for the person who did, your real frustration may be based on your inability to cope, which could show up just as easily in a nonfinancial situation. Your frustration dream that featured you missing the boat (or train or plane) or even your incompletion of the sex act would actually be your subconscious reminding you that certain traits of yours should be weeded out, or certain qualities developed to be able to cope. In other words, you may tend to blame a person or circumstance, when really the fault lies in yourself.

Passive Dreams Not really your style of dream, nor are you apt to experience them very often. These are the dreams in which you are the objective watcher of the action, not feeling the emotions or reactions of the dream sequence, but observing it as it unfolds before your eyes. You see yourself almost as a separate entity rather than as *you.* The purpose of the passive dream is to teach the dreamer to be detached from emotion-laden situations, to see the picture in its totality rather than in its particular frame of reference from the ego standpoint. Sagittarians are capable of being pretty objective in waking hours, tending to take the "large view" of life and not to get bound up in distracting side issues. Therefore, if you are a typical Sagittarian, you do not have the subconscious need for this type of dream as do people of some of the other signs. You can still benefit from it, of course, as the passive dream can present you with extra little pointers about the possible motives of other individuals as revealed in their actions or comments in the dream.

Action Dreams This is more your style! In the action dream you are getting going—on your way to or from a specific place—or you are climbing stairs or running for a moving vehicle (and boarding it). You may be participating in a sport, where you really feel the swing of the golf club or tennis racquet, or the motion of your rushing body if it's a competitive speed sport. There is often a sense of urgency in the action dream and sometimes of exhilaration as you figuratively hurl yourself toward an objective and attain it. This sort of dream is in tune with your temperament, and if the action or its aftermath is not unpleasant, shows that you have recently made—or are about to make—a definite decision in some area of your life. The physical activity in your dream is symbolic of decisive action in real life. If the dream is enjoyable, you are subconsciously reflecting in your dream your feeling of accomplishment in having taken a step toward a desired goal. As a fire-sign person, your attitude is that almost any action is better than *no* action. However, if you find the dream activity wearing or painful, or if you awaken exhausted from it, there is a real-life counterpart of your dream action theme that could bear analysis.

Recurring Dreams The recurring dream may pop up

every so often or merely two or three times in your life. It may be an exact duplicate each time you dream it, or so similar in theme and details that you experience a sense of familiarity with it—a "here we go again" reaction. This type of dream is trying to tell you something; or, rather, your subconscious is using this dream format to get a point across. If the dream doesn't seem to make any sense at all and if you can't take it at its face value and relate it to something in your life (a situation, relationship, or one of your own traits or viewpoints), then you must examine the symbolism in your recurring dream. The person about whom you dream may not be important in his or her own character, but might represent another individual. To take a rather hackneyed example, but one which points up the procedure, if you have a recurring dream in which an older man presents a problem (it could be a boss, teacher, neighbor, or friend), this mature male could be a father image and the message of this particular dream may be to reexamine your relationship with your father or settle a problem concerning him. In other words, people are not always whom they seem to be in your dreams, so if you have a recurring dream, and if the individual(s) in it or the environment or the plot are not pertinent to any condition in your current life, then delve deeper and correlate the dream with an analogous reality.

Escape Dreams One of everyone's favorite dreams, especially yours! The keynote of the escape dream is that you are, obviously, "escaping" from something unpleasant or restrictive to a condition that's free and enjoyable. The ultimate in escape dreams is when you are flying (on your own, not enclosed in a plane). Though this is sometimes given a sexual connotation, unless the dream is complex and fraught with other symbolism, this dream simply is your subconscious desire to escape your problems, burdens, responsibilities. Launching yourself off the earth and into free nonrestrictive space is often an acting out in dream episode of a subconscious fantasy of total escape from earth-related problems such as the need for money, food, clothing, or shelter. Other forms of escape dream may feature a sunny clime, less wearing apparel, or you may sprint mightily and just catch that last plane to Madrid! Or you drive off in a fast car, or exit through a door and slam it (with finality) behind you. From this sort of dream, one tends to awaken refreshed, exhilarated, filled with extra zest to cope with the day's problems. This is the purpose of a nice, enjoyable escape dream, which is produced by your subconscious wish to escape—and also by an inner need to have the pressure valve opened a bit. An especially Sagittarian sort of escape dream finds you on a high place—a hilltop, a roof, or on a circus high wire—where you revel in your top-spot position as you laugh down at the onlookers. Although you Sagittarians are not as center-stage-oriented as, for example, Leo people, your dreams do tend to find you attracting attention, usually because of some feat of daring that your subconscious desire for adventure dramatizes in dreams.

Sex Dreams In the first place, your waking-hours attitude toward sex is important and sometimes tends to carry over into the dream state. If you're a typical Sagittarian, sex is but one of life's many pleasures that you greatly enjoy. You tend to be well balanced sexually, neither overdoing your interest in the subject nor underplaying its importance. Basically, a person whose waking-hours sex life is both active and satisfying will experience fewer sex dreams than those individuals who are sexually "deprived." The sex drive is really a simple, uncomplicated drive, though people tend to complicate it greatly. In much the same way that you enjoy good food, good company, good conversation, and the good life in general, you tend to enjoy sex. You are not the type to approach sex with grim intensity or dreary obsessiveness. Consequently, in your sex dreams there is likely to be a lighthearted touch, just as there is in real life. With regard to your dream sex partners, flirt that you are, you may experience sexual attraction to "unattainable" people (mates of friends, for example) of whom you will dream sexually. In this kind of dream you will enjoy yourself tremendously, with no qualms upon awakening. In brief, sex to a Sagittarian is fun—one of life's major pleasures—but unless modifying factors in your individual birth chart show otherwise, sex is not a subject that messes up your psyche!

Sensuous Dreams These dreams involve especially strong impressions of one or more of the senses: seeing, hearing, smelling, tasting, touching. In such a dream, the vague, unsubstantial quality found in many dreams is lacking, replaced by a keen awareness of whatever the sense involved. The colors you see are vivid, unforgettable; the sounds permeate the air around you; the scents are strong, identifiable, memorable; the taste sensations are decidedly flavorful; the objects you touch are virtually real in texture. For a Sagittarian, such dreams can be your subconscious prodding you to develop further your creative talents. If the dreams are pleasant, they can also represent your sense of appreciation for a specific incident, such as a monetary gain, an honor, falling madly in love, or your appreciation of life in general—a quality strong in the Sagittarian.

In the event your sensuous dream is unpleasant, the interpretation is different, though again the dream usually reflects a message from your subconscious. If you dream of clashing, unharmonious colors or other visually disturbing subjects, your judgment is currently a bit off-center. Consider a real-life situation in which you have made or are about to make a judgment—and consider it further. If you dream of jangling, abrasive sounds, you are not at peace with yourself for some reason that probably relates to your environment (perhaps not enough room, a personality clash with an associate, or a running argument with someone). If, in your dream, there is an unpleasant smell, there is definitely something corrupt in your life: subterfuge, dishonesty, malice, or bad motivation in business or another relationship. You or the other person may be the guilty party, but this dream strongly suggests you revise your modus operandi (if it's you) or watch out for the other fellow. If your sensuous dream finds you becoming ill or awakening with a feeling of nausea (assuming that this does not stem from actual gastric upset), the message is obvious. You are overindulging one of your senses, not necessarily the sense of taste, but in one of your current sensuous waking patterns you are upsetting the fine balance between enough and too much. The tactile dream in which you are touching, holding, squeezing, stroking, or otherwise manually handling an object means there is need for you to evaluate a current matter. The tactile dream is the equivalent of pinching the avocado to see if it's ripe. Evaluate the progress, condition, or desirability of something to which you correlate this type of sensuous dream.

Precognitive Dreams You are a natural for this type of dream, in which subsequent happenings bear out the dream preview. Incidentally, you Sagittarians are especially prone to hearing voices in your precognitive dreams, but the voices you hear are not of the average dream quality in which someone says, "Hello, how are you?" and you answer, "I'm fine, how are you?" You'll know the precognitive dream voice when you hear it, for it has a recorded quality—a real-life voice that does not sound exactly real, but more like a radio or TV announcer. These audible dreams will be most significant, and even if you cannot adequately translate the message or meaning, this "voice" is calling your attention to something. This may herald a precognitive experience in your waking hours or perhaps a subsequent dream, but the point is to make you receptive to the precognitive experience. Inasmuch as you Sagittarians are not at all given to mystical feelings or seeing omens, you tend to accept your precognitive abilities matter-of-factly. Your precognitive experiences are seldom accompanied by emotion, but instead seem to pop into your head from out of the blue. In any case, you usually handle your precognitive dreams (or waking-hours precognitive experiences) sensibly, by neither overreacting nor cynically dismissing them as coincidence. Your problem may be in relating such dreams to subsequent happenings. There are two types of precognitive dreams: the exact dream which is duplicated in reality shortly afterward, or the dream in which the essence or theme provides the clue—good or bad news, elation or dejection, and so on. You tend to dream the latter. When you've had a few precognitive dreams and found that they later indeed do come true in essentials if not in details, then you learn to recognize them as you dream them instead of having to wait for their waking-hours confirmation. It is even possible that you have experienced precognitive dreams and not paid much attention to them, for the fact of the matter is that some of these dreams do not seem to be relevant to anything. (How important can it be when you dream that you receive a phone call from an old friend, and then you do receive a phone call from the friend, who has nothing very important to say anyway?) But in such an instance your subconscious is showing that you are tuned in to the cosmic stream, and that you can develop this gift. The result will be heightened spiritual awareness and/or a greater capacity for creative expression.

Peopled Dreams Everyone dreams of other people sometimes. In your case, it's fairly frequent, though people in your dreams tend to appear as faceless masses rather than specific individuals. In one way, this shows your sense of at-one-ness with the rest of mankind, reflected in your everyday life through your friendly, companionable manner. In another way, it reflects your reluctance to become too closely bound up with individuals. Your subconscious presents you with a group of individuals in your dream who are unlikely to make the demands on you that one person might. In dreams of specific people, if they are recognizable but are behaving out of character (your freewheeling bar buddy suddenly showing up as a man of the cloth, or gentle Sandra next door coming on like Ms. Lib), then you have to seek the correlation between the dream figure and the individual he or she represents. For instance, you dream of an elderly relative looking like an eighteen-year-old and dancing through the night. While this *might* be a forerunner of that relative's about-face on a certain issue, it is more likely to mean that someone you know in real life who has similar qualities and even a physical resemblance to the relative is the individual on whom the dream really focuses. Then there is also the possibility that one of those dream people may be a projection of you yourself. This is particularly to be noted when the dream person is behaving badly or is being chastised for something. Your subconscious wish is to spare yourself feelings of guilt or unpleasant experiences, so your subconscious gets around this by projecting you in another's form in the dream.

Symbols in Dreams You probably see lots of symbols in your dreams. In fact, as you will have noted, dreams generally contain much symbolism. Every once in a while you dream of a particular object or condition that seems especially symbolic and probably is. To dream of an item set off by itself—for example, a tree, a single rose, a pitcher, or a key—is symbolic of a real-life corollary. The door can mean an opportunity; the key, the solution to a problem; the single rose, a love attraction. Astrologically meaningful are dreams of the elements: fire, earth, air, or water. Fire represents the spirit, earth, the material body; air, the mind; water, the emotions. The element of fire is particularly significant for you, as yours is a fire sign. A dream involving pleasing, controlled fire (the fireplace, stove, lighted match) symbolizes not only your spiritual growth and potential but also the creative spark. Fire-related dreams and air-related dreams are compatible with your temperament and show that your subconscious is supportive of your efforts to expand your spiritual and creative potential. The symbolic value of dreaming of an animal depends on your feelings toward animals. If you like them, animal dreams signify friends, maybe love objects; if you dislike or fear them, dreaming of an animal can mean there's a person currently in your life about whom you have ambiguous feelings and whom you probably mistrust. If you should dream of the number six, the color purple, or the Centaur (the half-man, half-beast symbol of your sign), that dream can be very significant, for your subconscious is spotlighting, through symbolism, your true identity, possibly even your real mission in life. Actually, large animals are ruled by Sagittarius, so whether or not you like large animals (particularly horses) in real life, this animal can be symbolically important.

Chapter 13

Capricorn

(December 22–January 20)

Your natural instincts stem from your unconscious, while your innermost desires lie in the realm of your subconscious. Your Sun sign is the essential you, through which your instincts and desires are expressed in an individualistic and unique fashion. Because you are a Capricorn your dreams reflect, in their contents and meaning, this individualism.

CAPRICORN is an Earth sign, ruled by Saturn, cardinal in quality (which means action-oriented). The combination of cardinality with the earth element is reflected in your temperament, for you are exceedingly practical, with a fine sense of material values (Earth), as well as ambitious and quick to take advantage of opportunity to further your position in life. However, while you are indeed quick to follow up on an opportunity, the association of Saturn with your sign sometimes makes such opportunities rather hard to come by, as we are sure you will agree! While of course there are exceptions, usually nothing comes too easily or too quickly to a Capricorn. Fortunately Saturn has also endowed you with patience and the willingness to work hard for your goals, and the obstacles and delays you sometimes encounter do not at all dim your basic ambition. Though money and other material badges of success are high on your list of priorities (as with all Earth-sign people) you aim, perhaps even more strongly, for recognition. Deep in the Capricorn soul is the theory that credit should be given where credit is due! You also lust a bit for power, whether this is directed toward community or political goals (in which areas, incidentally, you are a natural) or in the bosom of your family, where you are the one who gives the instructions and makes the decisions. Or, it could be in your business or professional career, in which you gravitate toward an executive position. You are a good manager of funds, projects, and other people's lives. You can also manage your own life in exemplary fashion, provided you make positive use of your traits and talents, for you can be self-disciplined, well-organized, and objective in your thinking. The Saturnian influence inclines you toward a bit of formality on occasion, a respect for tradition and established principles, and shows up in your basic conservatism. You also have an off-beat sense of humor, and are far more emotional and sensitive than your innate reserve permits you to display.

Your Unconscious Instincts You have strong urges to attain and to organize. Translated into everyday living, this means you are oriented toward improving your position in life, attaining status, authority, respect, material success. To this purpose you organize your life style and modus operandi, map out your plans and strategies, and, early in life, decide on your priorities. Your eye is ever on the main goal, from which it is not too easy to divert you. Timing is also important to you and you are inclined to allot specific time spans for achieving special goals (subject, always, to Saturnian delays, of course, but you know this well and take it into consideration in your plans). An example might be the Capricorn man who decides that marriage is on his agenda—but not until he reaches a certain point of achievement in career or finances. You Capricorns are great believers that "for everything there is a season and a time for every purpose."

Sometimes you can be a bit rigid with regard to your schedule, whether it's the daily routine of breakfast at eight, to the corner bus at eight forty-five, seated at your desk by nine thirty, and lunch at one o'clock sharp, or the larger schedule of your mapped-out life plan. You tend to be a clock watcher, literally and figuratively, but not for the reason that many people are. You do not keep track of the time in order to dash away from labor to pleasure, carefully avoiding giving one extra minute of work to the company. You watch the clock to make sure you are on time, on schedule, in rhythm with the well-organized agenda you set for yourself.

Your urge to attain is somewhat different from the desire to achieve, possess, accomplish, though it has elements of these three, too. To attain means "to arrive at" and this subtle distinction relates to your keen awareness of status and position in life. True, money, possessions, and accomplishments help to assure status, but they do not guarantee it. To be a person of influence in your career or community, to have a voice that is listened to in high places, to receive a certain amount of deference and respect from both colleagues and subordinates—that is your idea of "arriving at" the position you want. While you relish being a power in such ways, you are not one to abuse power, to come on too strong, to want to run the whole show. In fact, you can be exceedingly impartial in your treatment of and attitude toward other people. In other words, you are gracious in your use of power. There is one thing, though, that anyone close to you learns fast. Whether it's your family, co-workers, or employees, you expect them to perform. No slacking off on the work schedule where you are involved. You work hard and expect others to do the same! Your unconscious instincts can be recognized, nurtured, and redirected into positive expression when necessary by an act of the conscious will. These instincts are constantly operative, whether you are awake or asleep, where they form a background to your dreams. However, the majority of your dreams are produced by . . .

Your Subconscious Desires Subconsciously, you desire security and recognition, and many of your actions reflect these subconscious motivations. Since the majority of you Capricorns have had to learn to work hard for your money, you not only know the value of a dollar but tend to make long-range preparations to ensure an adequate supply of dollars for your old age. (Even Capricorns who are born into wealthy families tend to be blessed with the kind of parents who impress upon them the fact that money does not grow on trees!) As a result, material security is important to you, and while you are capable of spending freely when it comes to social entertaining, where formal elegance is your style, and to business expenditures (where you spend money to make money), in your personal life and habits you can be rather austere. Certainly you don't fling cash around like a Leo or Sagittarian. You can "make do" as well as do without if your incentive is to build up your financial security.

Emotional security is also important to you, perhaps more vital to your welfare than you may think. Your tendency to act according to a schedule may prompt you to postpone involvement with someone until such time as it shows up on your list of priorities. However, once you do marry (and marriage is invariably included in your plans, for despite any passing phases of no-ties permissiveness Capricorn is basically drawn to conservative tradition), you find that emotional security has, indeed, been a need for you all along.

Because of your desire for security, your waking

hours feature a lot of planning and activity directed toward achieving it. But this particular desire, a strong one, also shows up in your subconscious and in your dreams. You have to admit, Capricorn, that you do have a tendency to anticipate the worst. Your theory is that it's better to expect the worst and then be pleasantly surprised if it doesn't happen, then it is to expect the best and be disappointed. Accordingly, your worries and anticipation of dire events sometimes become vivid panoramas of doom and gloom! Especially in matters of material security, where you may envision yourself winding up like the Little Match Girl in fable, or flat broke and hungry, at the same time that you are stashing away money like mad. Time is ever on the side of Capricorns, however, and your later years are very often much easier than your early ones.

Your desire for recognition is based primarily on your strong sense of justice, whereby credit is given for good deeds performed. It is especially difficult for you Capricorns to do good anonymously and to eschew the public acclamation you feel is due you. On the other hand, you are scrupulously honest and will not accept undeserved plaudits. As a matter of fact, that word "deserve" (very Saturnian, as this planet is associated with Karma, the law of cause and effect) is central to your vocabulary. You do believe people should get what they deserve, nothing more and nothing less, and you feel exceptionally strong about this when you are the one who *deserves* the recognition you desire.

These subconscious desires for security and recognition can manifest in your dreams particularly if your waking hours are not producing much of either. Insecurity and frustration dreams, or recurring dreams with an especially worrisome theme, might plague you until you identify the specific sources of your insecurity. Once you recognize and face up to them, you are quite capable of organizing your forces to remedy them with true Capricorn efficiency.

Your Special Talents and Abilities These belong in the area of your conscious state, your waking-hours awareness. You undoubtedly know that you have certain talents. You may not, as yet, be aware of some of your latent talents and abilities, for Capricorns sometimes are late bloomers and do not fully develop all their potential until maturity. Some of your special abilities are based on character traits inherent in your nature, which are actively expressed as the occasion demands: your patience, your ability to work hard, to work long hours, and to meticulously discharge your duties. It's not that you are basically a patient person, like Taurus; patience is something you develop and utilize when you see that eventually it will pay off. You have to see that light at the end of the tunnel in order to continue your patient plodding toward a goal. "Plodding" is not a very exciting word, perhaps, but the result of your particular kind of plodding can bring exciting rewards in due time. This ties in with your ability to be super efficient in whatever you do, whether or not you really enjoy doing it. If, for example, you have your eye on being the president of a company, or heading a major department in the firm, you are able to start at the bottom, master every boring little detail of the work, patiently work long hours, and wait in the wings until the time comes for advancement. Only then do you move very rapidly, indeed, to take advantage of the opportunity. You are then in a position, having worked your way up through the ranks, to be an extremely efficient and knowledgeable boss. In other words, your ability to work, plod, and patiently persevere is based on expedience. You adapt your methods to achieve a particular goal. The goal must be there, and attainable, in order for you to utilize your many abilities.

Of all the zodiacal types, you are probably the one with the greatest ability to be self-disciplined, self-denying. Again, there has to be the incentive for it. Some people are naturally self-disciplined, naturally oriented toward an austere life style, whether or not they have any particular goal in life. But you Capricorns have the ability to *adapt* to such a routine and *adopt* it as the means to an end. Therefore, motive and incentive are all-important for you, since these are what activate your abilities.

With regard to your talents—well, they are considerable. Here, too, motivation and incentive are vital for the full development of your many talents. Because you are not among those who are turned off by the prospect of long years of training and education, Capricorns are numerous in the fields of law, medicine, education, science. Professional status may mean as much to you as the income it brings. But because you are business-oriented as well, you also have a decided flair for any commercial enterprise that has big-money potential. You are particularly talented in "selling" to the general public, though not necessarily as a salesperson. You have a sort of sixth sense in knowing, for example, what the trend of consumer buying will be, whether a certain product should be promoted immediately, or whether it will go over better six months or a year from now. Timing, again, plays its part in your business/financial objectives.

Your sense of timing, your harmony with cosmic rhythms, also makes many a Capricorn a fine musician. Here, too, you will not mind the long hours of practice, for it is particularly satisfying for you not only to master the intricacies of a musical instrument, but to know that by so doing you will be able to attain a secure niche in the field of music, to say nothing of being able to command high fees.

Another of your talents relates to the Earth quality of Capricorn. You may be a productive gardener, and could be successful in the nursery business, in agriculture, or in the field of ecology. Related to the planet Earth, too, are jobs and professions in land development, real estate, mining, or construction, and you Capricorns have special talents in these areas as well.

Both astrology and dreams are aids in helping you to realize your potential by using your talents and abilities. This theme should appeal to you, for you have an inherent urge to make use of whatever you have or whatever comes your way. It may be, though, that at this point you have yet to make maximum use of your assets. If that is the case, you should do a bit of self-analysis—and dream analysis. For if you have tended to coast along, without much motivation or incentive, your dreams will surely reflect this. If you're a square peg in a round hole in your work, social life, or leisure activities, you are likely to have many a confinement or frustration dream. On the other hand, once you find your real identity and are decisive about specific goals in life, everyday frustrations or restrictions tend to roll off your back like water off a duck, for you've got your motivation, you've got your incentive, and you've got your patience-and-hard-work habit going for you. You will also experience more relaxing and inspirational dreams.

What Specific Dream Categories Mean to You

Confinement Dreams This is the dream where you are either physically or mentally confined. You are literally locked in a room or some other vague, unknown place from which you cannot escape, or your mental inertia is so great that you are unable to move, call for help, or even think. In this dream, you are tied or bound in one way or another, and though your only objective is to get out of the situation, you continue to be confined in it (until you awaken, or the dream scene makes one of those sudden changes). Sometimes confinement dreams have a nightmare quality, with some person about to hurt or kill you (usually a total stranger!) or a sense of impending doom throughout. In the first place, this latter kind of confinement dream should not be interpreted as a forerunner of a dire event. The confinement in the dream simply reflects a confinement condition in your waking hours. More importantly, it represents a confinement situation within yourself. Invariably the confinement is self-imposed—whether it stems from a sense of restriction involving your job, family life, personal relationships, or financial state—or from an inhibition in *you* that prevents you from "breaking out" into a more fulfilling life style. In your dream, you are stuck there (wherever you are) and cannot get out—which is your subconscious advising you quite pointedly that there you will remain unless you take the reins in your hands and do something about it! Capricorns who are not really utilizing their talents and abilities will tend to experience this type of dream. In one way it reflects some of the inhibiting factors in the Capricorn nature, but in another it also reflects the lethargy that sometimes sets in when you do not really know where you're going.

The confinement dream can also stem from something specific currently happening in your life. Perhaps through your own words or actions you got yourself into a bind and can see no way out at the moment. You may have antagonized an important person, or double-crossed a friend, or not been generous when you could have been. The estrangement or the remorse you feel as a result of your actions is expressed in your dream, where you are confined by a web of your own making. Once the matter is set straight, this sort of confinement dream fades away.

Insecurity Dreams You may be especially prone to insecurity dreams; but then, who isn't? It's the most common of all dreams and is identified by an experience of loss, lack, or search. In this dream you've misplaced your purse or wallet (with all your life savings in it!), or your car is missing, or your attaché case with vital material you are taking somewhere. It may be your child, or a loved pet, or a valuable possession that's missing. Sometimes you spend what seems to be the whole night searching for the lost item—waking up before you ever find it. In any case, the impression this dream leaves with you is one of great insecurity and much anxiety. This, of course, can reflect almost any day-to-day situation or happening, as there are certainly numerous seeds of insecurity around us all. More specifically, you may feel a bit worried about your job or a financial deal, not a full-blown waking-hours worry, but a tinge of anxiety that's tucked away in your subconscious, and here it is dominating your dream. Usually, but not always, if you lose a material object in your dream, it represents insecurity about a material matter. If it is a person who is among the missing in your dream, it could represent emotional insecurity in your waking hours. Sometimes, though, these rules are reversed and you can determine this by your dream reaction. For example, if in your dream you are weeping copiously and feel that your heart is broken because a wallet with a few dollars is gone, this would be an emotional insecurity masked in a material object. The insecurity dream can also feature you wearing very little clothing in some situation where you should certainly be dressed: a party, dinner, the main street of your city. This represents your subconscious fear of being exposed for something you've done or failed to do. The fact that in your partially clothed or nude insecurity dream no one else even notices your physical exposure also indicates that your failing has not come to light as yet, but you fear that it will. It may be quite a minor thing: a bit of gossip that you fear may be traced to you, or a slightly off-center business transaction, or a white lie you told. You Capricorns can be scrupulous about this sort of thing, and it's your own reaction to having done this deed, not the actual importance of it, that shows up in the dream.

Frustration Dreams Another Capricorn special! Particularly if you are not happy in your work or with your general life style, or if you are floundering about, not yet having found your direction in life. In this dream, the hallmark is incompletion, whether it's you on your way to someplace at which you never arrive, or the interruption of your announcing or receiving important news, or an incompleted sex act, or your mad dash for a train or bus that's just left. In the frustration dream it appears as though some outside circumstances interfere with the completion of whatever you set out to do. Actually, though, the frustration dream can represent self-doubts—perhaps you feel you will be unable (in your waking hours) to prove yourself on the new job, make a success of the party you're planning, hold your new lover, or come up with the funds for a major bill. Your subconscious tends to direct any sort of blame or guilt away from you—which is quite logical, inasmuch as most of us are not truly objective, but tend to rationalize and spare ourselves the full responsibility of any problem. Accordingly, the subconscious often projects that blame or guilt on others in dreams, or in dream circumstances, where you ran fast but the train left, or you tried to impart information but others wouldn't listen, and so on. So the frustration dream *can* be a reflection of your own timidity, lack of confidence, or failure to be aggressive. Once you identify the waking-hours source of your frustration—whether it is indeed a certain condition in your life, or your own failure to cope with it—then you bring it out into the light of day where you can outline your plans and strategies for handling the matter.

Passive Dreams This is the dream that could be described as a panoramic view of things, where you observe the action but do not participate. You see yourself, as though you were another person, proceeding through the dream plot, while you, as the observer, do not seem to have a vested interest in the proceedings, but are merely an onlooker. The message of this dream concerns objectivity and comprehensive thinking. In other words, there is some situation in your life in which you are too caught up on a personal level, and this emotional involvement has distorted your sense of perspective. This type of dream can enable you to take a broader view of the matter and may also provide clues as to what's going on in the part of the plot in which you are not directly involved. For instance, you may be immersed in a personality clash with a co-worker, and because your emotions are involved you may tend to be overly sensitive or overly suspicious. Your passive dream could feature a group of people (not necessarily even including the real-life co-worker) who are very relaxed and friendly, welcoming you to their midst. Inasmuch as the passive dream is bringing the message of objectivity, and inasmuch as this dream features a friendly group, the interpretation would be that others in your job surroundings couldn't care less about the personal "feud" to which you have given so much importance, that they think well of you, and that it's possible you have made a mountain out of a molehill because of your intensely personal involvement in the situation. Relate whatever emotionally biased situation exists in your waking hours to your passive dream and you will begin to see things more objectively.

Action Dreams These are quite the reverse of the passive dream, for you are explicitly involved in decisive action, usually physical. You may be walking fast, running, leaping, climbing stairs, carrying heavy packages (and literally feeling their weight), or performing any other definite action in which you experience full participation. This sort of dream is easy to interpret, for it represents real-life action—not necessarily of a physical nature, but rather in terms of making a firm decision, starting a project, or settling a problem. Upon awakening from an action dream, you usually feel full of vim and vigor as this sort of dream is often the prelude to your taking decisive action in a real-life situation. However, if the dream action is unpleasant or exhausting, it means you should further explore the possible results of your contemplated waking-hours action. For instance, you may be considering taking on additional work of some sort or heading up a community project (a typical Capricorn action), and if your dream features you running up the stairs and becoming more and more tired as you ascend—or carrying those heavy packages, which become more and more of a burden—then your subconscious is reminding you to consider how you are going to squeeze in this additional activity with all your other responsibilities. On the other hand, though the stairs may be steep or the packages heavy, your dream reaction may be that you can handle it with a little extra effort; in this case, your contemplated waking-hours decisive action would probably be equally easy to handle.

Recurring Dreams These are dreams that you have over and over again. Sometimes people experience the recurring dream only a few times in their lives, or it can come more frequently. The recurring dream may be an exact repeat in every detail each time it is dreamed or it may be so similar in outline, plot, and your reactions to it, that you have the sensation you've been there before. Obviously, there is an important meaning in a dream that keeps popping up. It may relate to a long-standing condition in your life or to a long-held conviction or aim of yours. In either case, the condition or conviction could bear examining, because something about it is not right (or you would not have the recurring dream). Pay attention to a person who appears in such a dream, even though, in dream fashion, the person may not be whom he or she seems to be. The figure in your dream may be an "image" of someone else or even you yourself as projected by your subconscious. Analogy is sometimes present in the recurring dream. For example, in the dream you may be clasping your childhood doll or teddy bear, or talking with a friend from the distant past, or weeping over a lost love. In other words, the theme may relate to the past and the meaning of the dream could be that it's time to let go of old comforts (such as a self-indulgent habit), old prejudices, or old sorrows. That is merely an example, but do look for symbolic meanings as well as concrete clues in your recurring dreams. You Capricorns tend to retain links with the past, which is a positive trait when it concerns sound principles, standards, established ideals, but negative if it prompts you to rehash old grievances or brood over old disappointments.

Escape Dreams The escape dream features your getting out of a restrictive situation and into one where freedom prevails. This can take the form of a semi-nightmare in which an evil person or unidentified thing is pursuing you, though you manage to get away before you wake up. Or it can be the sort of dream where you exit from a door and step into a new and much happier environment. The escape dream can see you running for a bus or train and boarding it (at which point your dream reaction is that now your problems are over and you've made it!), or maybe you actually leave the ground and fly away, totally on your own and not in a plane. That is one of the most enjoyable kinds of escape dreams, for you soar over the heads of the earth-bound (who usually pay no attention whatsoever to your strange feat) and feel that you are the master or mistress of all you survey. In any case, the escape dream represents your subconscious need for freedom from responsibilities, burdens, work, unhappiness, or whatever is bothering you most. This kind of dream has a beneficial effect, too, for upon awakening you invariably feel energetic, confident, and better able to cope with the day's demands. These dreams have therapeutic value, and there should be more of them! You Capricorns would tend to experience the escape dream when you really need it, as it represents your subconscious lessening the pressures of life, if only for a brief dream episode. Although you can take more pressure than many people can, still an occasional escape into the wild blue yonder (or whatever your dream highlights) is well deserved.

Sex Dreams In general, people whose waking-hours sex lives are both active and satisfying do not tend to experience unusually many sex dreams. However, those Capricorns who are totally involved with career, money-making, or public life can, in fact, ignore sex for fairly long periods of time, and tend to experience sex dreams as a result. Repressed desires that are tucked away in the subconscious will also surface in dreams, sometimes surprisingly. Invariably, the partner of your sex dream is decidedly not the partner you desire or have been attracted to, however slightly. The partner in your sex dream, though, would have something in common with a real-life attraction, if only in terms of general physical type, age, or life style. Your sexual attraction to someone whose work involves dealing with the public (a receptionist, bank teller, policeman, salesperson) could result in a sex dream with a vaguely similar type, but with the action taking place in full view of a crowd (very embarrassing to a Capricorn!). Or you might be sexually attracted to a mature person or a very young individual and find that your dream sex partner is in one of those age groups. Unless you have specific hang-ups about sex, however, you'll find that sex dreams, or the absence of them, reflect the degree of your waking-hours sexual fulfillment.

Sensuous Dreams These are dreams highlighted by your acute awareness that you are exercising one of the five senses: sight, hearing, smell, taste, or touch. In many dreams you are in situations where the senses are involved, but you do not experience their reality. You may dream you're out to dinner, but not taste the food, or you might dream you're in a garden, but there is no scent of the flowers or shrubs. In the sensuous dream, however, you actually partake of the sensation—colors are vivid, every detail of a person's face or clothing is noted, the sound you hear is really audible, scents are pungent, food is flavored with identifiable spices, and the object or material in your fingers seems even more real than in life. If the sensation in these dreams is pleasing it represents your satisfaction regarding a recent waking-hours accomplishment or event. If the sensation is unpleasant, it may reflect a real-life disappointment, or it could also be your subconscious cautioning you against overindulgence or misuse of one of your senses.

The sense of touch is particularly Capricornian as this is symbolic of evaluation (much in the same manner as you feel the yard goods before buying it, or hold a fruit or vegetable in your hand to determine its weight, juiciness, and so on). If you should have a sensuous dream in which you are touching, stroking, or feeling an object, it might refer to a waking-hours situation or plan you are assessing. It can also refer to a plan or proposed course of action that you *should* be evaluating but are not.

The sense of taste generally relates to one's appetite for food or drink. You Capricorn people can have big appetites and really enjoy eating and drinking, although you also have that previously mentioned ability for self-discipline when tempted to overindulge. A dream featuring the sense of taste could provide you with meaningful clues.

Precognitive Dreams Capricorn people in general are reluctant to take anything on faith alone. "Show me" is a demand frequently stated or intimated by you sensible types, so yours is not a sign that's noted for its unquestioning acceptance of anything occult. Precognitive dreams come under that category, for in such dreams one is temporarily tuned in to cosmic timelessness and is able to catch a glimpse of the future. The precognitive dream is one which, shortly thereafter, "comes true" in a real-life happening, either in exact detail or in essence. For example, to dream of a kitten you were given when you were fifteen, and two days later your mate comes home with a puppy would be precognitive in essence because in each instance you received an animal. Or, you might dream you received a letter with Argentinian stamps and postmark, and a few days later you *do* receive a letter with Argentinian stamps and postmark. That would be precognitive in detail. You may have experienced a precognitive dream or two in your life and written it off as coincidence, especially since the subject matter of such dreams is frequently not all that important. The main point of such dreams, though, is that your subconscious is reminding you that you do have spiritual awareness, an upper-plane perceptivity that you may or may not wish to develop further. If you do have dreams that subsequently are mirrored in real-life events, you should of course pay attention to this special "gift."

Peopled Dreams Many an individual walks through our dreams, and sometimes crowds of people appear. As a Capricorn, you would tend to dream of groups, even masses of people (though of course you would also dream of individuals as well). The presence of groups of people in your dreams represents, on one level, your fellow man, with whom you tend to be involved in terms of competition (you against *them*, vying for a place in the sun), instruction (you teaching, advising, or directing *them*), or performance (you being the performer, *they* the audience). This can reflect Capricorn's rather impersonal approach to people in general, as opposed to those born under other signs of the Zodiac who tend to become personally involved and who identify emotionally with others. On another level, your dreaming of groups of people represents your need for others in your life. You Capricorns can sometimes be solitary folk, convinced that you are pretty self-sufficient. Your subconscious is providing you with people, lots of them, as a symbol of the companionship you need. When you dream of specific individuals, they may not be the people they appear to be—particularly if they are behaving out of character. The person in your dream may be a projection of yourself, or of someone who generally resembles or acts like the dream figure. Once you realize the varied possibilities for matching real-life situations and people with those in your dreams, you can more easily identify the meanings of your nightly dream excursions.

Symbols in Dreams Many dreams are highly symbolic, but occasionally you will have a dream that particularly accentuates an object or pattern—perhaps a color, number, animal, tree, a single flower, or maybe a mountain (this last being very significant for a Capricorn, as your symbol, the Mountain Goat, is headed for that peak!). Astrologically, the elements are very symbolic. Fire represents the spirit; earth, the material body; air, the mind; and water, the emotions. A dream of earthy matters (gardening, planting, and sowing—other Capricornian symbolisms—or walking through meadows or countryside) can be, especially in a pleasant dream, an affirmation of your basic strengths and assets. If it is an unpleasant dream, your subconscious is trying to get you back on the right path. Earth- and water-related dreams are compatible with your temperament and concern your need to realize your full potential. The significance of dreaming of animals will depend on your waking-hours feelings about them. If you like animals, dreaming of one can represent a good friend, a wise judgment you've made, or perhaps a love object. If you dislike, fear, or are indifferent to animals, dreaming of one can signify a relationship you are questioning, an associate you suspect has ulterior motives, or a matter on which you are reserving judgment until more facts are available. If you should dream of the number four, the color indigo blue, or a horned animal (especially the Goat) that dream will be significant, for it focuses on your true identity and may provide clues as to your mission in life and how to achieve it.

Chapter 14

Aquarius

(January 21–February 19)

Your natural instincts flow from your unconscious, while your deepest desires are in the realm of your subconscious. Your Sun sign represents your own unique individuality, through which are expressed these natural instincts and subconscious desires. Because you are an Aquarian your dreams reflect this individuality of yours, both in content and meaning.

AQUARIUS is an air sign, ruled by Uranus, fixed in quality (which means concentrated, unyielding). The combination of fixity with the air element is reflected in your temperament, and one of the reasons why you Aquarians are often described as unpredictable is that air and fixity are not compatible. At times you are as free as the summer breeze, at other times you are determinedly inflexible (and no one can predict what your mood will be at any given time). Although you're noted for your idealism and your vision (you are really tuned in to the future), as well as for your occasional impracticality, you can also be unexpectedly materialistic, worrying about money you've so casually spent, hesitant to step out of your secure little groove into the great unknown. You love personal freedom and independence, but sometimes you think and talk about it more than you actually do anything about achieving it. There are diverse pulls between staying where you are (fixity) and wanting to break free and soar (air). You have also been known to get some fixed idea in your mind, and no one—but no one—can talk you out of it! The association of Uranus with your sign gives you a unique sort of creativity and is also responsible for some of your off-beat interests, strange friendships, and that certain contrariness of reaction you display, which really throws people who thought they had you neatly categorized. Probably the best description of you Aquarians is to say that you actually cannot be described with any degree of certainty; you are constantly surprising all of us, and, we suspect, you often surprise yourself, too!

Your Unconscious Instincts You have strong urges to rebel and to invent. In a way, you might be called contrary, for just let the majority of people you know hold to a certain view, and you almost automatically take the opposite view. Although the revolution and anarchy popularly supposed to usher in the Age of Aquarius are but dramatic exaggerations to the average Aquarian, you do have your little manifestations of rebellion. It's really quite your natural reaction to question tradition, authority, or established procedure. You are the one who courteously asks the traffic cop *why* you must take the detour that everyone else is taking (and he may have a hard time convincing you why), or it could be you who makes an issue of some ordinance with which you do not agree. You may be a voice crying in the wilderness, but you don't hesitate to fight City Hall! You tend to cross against red lights, pleasantly speak up in public about some subject that everyone is assiduously avoiding, and you're a natural to start any sort of class-action suit.

Since most Aquarians have considerable personal charm and are innately courteous and considerate of others, it usually comes as a surprise when you are the one who sets off a big brouhaha. Since you are very often ahead of your time, it can be years before the fruits of your rebellion are seen, at which point people seldom remember that it was indeed an Aquarian who pointed the way. It is precisely because you are so future-oriented that your urge is to cut through the red tape or outworn traditions, to rebel now for better conditions later. This unconscious instinct shows up in many and varied ways, and because most people are pretty much preoccupied with the here and now, your future outlook as expressed in your rebellion against the status quo is quite naturally labeled contrariness and unpredictability. But you don't really care!

Aquarians have the urge to invent and many a patent has been issued to people of your sign. But you are mentally inventive, too, dazzling others with your creativity, originality, and off-beat sort of inspiration. Aquarians excel at devising theories, concepts, abstract principles. Sometimes these are workable, sometimes not, but one can be sure that your Aquarian mind will not follow along the groove of familiar, established, traditional thought patterns. In everyday life, your inventiveness finds expression in time-saving business or domestic procedures, blending unlikely or incompatible creative art forms into a brand new dimension, or giving fabulous parties with many a novel twist and not a dull moment!

Your unconscious instincts to rebel and to invent are constantly operative, whether you are awake or asleep. They can be recognized, nurtured, directed (or redirected) into positive expression by an act of your conscious will. They are also there in the background of your dreams. But the majority of your dreams are produced by . . .

Your Subconscious Desires Subconsciously, you desire to be independent and to express yourself with originality. These desires stem from your urge to rebel (an expression of independence) and to invent, as the very seed of inventiveness contains the imprint of originality. Your desire for independence is a two-way street, nicely balanced by your inclination to allow others as much independence as you yourself desire. This is fine when the people with whom you are closely associated or whom you marry have a similar attitude. But if you are closely involved with a person of a jealous or possessive nature, you could suffer a lot or break out of the situation, depending on how Uranian you are feeling at the moment. Also, a jealous, possessive person who happens to be in love with an Aquarian experiences his or her share of suffering, too, for of all the zodiacal types, you are the one most likely to arouse jealousy in another in a purely unintentional and usually quite innocent manner. For one thing, you are attracted to people who are stimulating and whose careers, ideas, creativity, or travels make them fascinating conversationalists. Secondly, your own personal charm and the enthusiastic attention you give such individuals combine to make it seem that you are personally and romantically attracted to them—when all the time it's the person's mind that intrigues you. Your jealous partner, of course, thinks the worst, resulting in a scene or confrontation (which you dislike) and emotional turmoil (which you dislike even more). The moral of this example is that you Aquarians should, for your own peace of mind, steer clear of jealous, possessive types, for you are basically so independent that you'll never be in the mood to conform to more restrictive behavior.

Your independence also shows up in your work methods, choice of career (an Aquarian not being one to count on to continue the family business), religious or political convictions, selection of friends, and leisure activities. Usually, you do not make a big thing out of going your own way, but simply do so in a calm, kindly, courteous manner.

Your desire to be original stems from your dissatisfaction with the limitations of tried and true methods, or with set patterns or any conformist situation. You are an avant-garde sort—way ahead of today's innovations and well into those of tomorrow. This can result in some excellent creative work, but also in some rather strange fashions or theories! Unlike your polar opposite, Leo, who is always aware of the audience reaction, your frequently dramatic expressions of originality stem from the desire to *be* original—not to be *seen* as original by others. Deep in the heart of every Aquarian is a fine disregard for what others may think or say, and this does flavor your desires for independence and originality in a most unique manner.

Your dreams, whether they are vague or definite, reveal your subconscious desires, and many of your dreams can be traced to your love of independence and originality. Because you are a creative person, as well as basically nonconformist, your dreams are likely to be either very vivid and memorable, or deeply buried the moment you awaken. You do not tolerate in-between vagueness, even in dreams! You would tend to dream in color a lot, as this is an indication of the creative mind, and your dreams would probably include much symbolism and numerous people. Because you Aquarians can be especially intuitive, you are probably the best translator of your own dreams.

Your Special Abilities and Talents These come under the category of your conscious state, your waking-hours awareness. Foremost among your abilities is that of dealing with people. While descriptions of your sign frequently mention humanitarianism as a prime quality of Aquarians, for the most part this is expressed in a very definite ability to relate to all kinds of people, from all walks of life. Very advanced Aquarians do, in fact, gravitate toward careers in which their work or ideas are beneficial to mankind, often dedicating their lives to humanitarian ideals. The average Aquarian, however, although he or she may be drawn to a career in medicine, education, or the social services, usually expresses a humanitarian instinct through general helpfulness to others. You do feel concern for your fellow man, but not an obsessive concern. You can be quite objective about other people's problems, and you do not try to impose your views or standards upon them. This ability of yours to relate to others in a friendly, detached, undemanding way, and to counsel them objectively, is an asset in both your personal and professional life. You also have the ability to see the end results of present activity. In other words, your future-oriented and uniquely Aquarian vision enables you to somehow *know* the outcome of a project, theory, strategy, or whatever. And even if people do not always listen to your "forecasting," as often as not time proves you right.

You may have a special ability for statistics, which might seem to be an odd talent for an Aquarian, but people of your sign often have a scientific instinct. Hence the interest in the process of amassing statistics, finding constant factors on which to determine a point, and utilizing such figures for a specific and well-defined purpose. Unless you are especially shy and introverted (which once in a while an Aquarian may be) you do well in extrovert situations, where you meet, greet, inform, or instruct people. Like Librans, you Aquarians can be the epitome of charm and diplomacy; the unique and unexpected facets of your personality draw people to you. In general, you are repelled by the nine-to-five routine or—for that matter—by routine, period. Having your own profession or business enterprise is much more to your liking, but unless you have already proven to yourself that you have a good business sense and can deal practically with finances, you should be somewhat cautious in sinking your hard-earned cash into a personally run commercial venture. You Aquarians are not noted for your down-to-earth practicality.

Your talents and abilities may equip you for a career in the arts. Aquarians are often popular writers, avant-garde artists, musicians, or actors. As a matter of fact, many of you really appeal to mass audiences—certainly an asset if you aim to be a film star, top pop singer, or TV personality. Actually, television and radio are rather typically Aquarian fields, whether you are in the limelight or working behind the scenes. Many of you also find satisfying careers in philanthropy, politics, and the space program (the last being the most Aquarian field of all).

As you will have noted, you've a great selection of choices when it comes to how best to use your special talents and abilities—which, of course, can be either utilized or neglected. Sometimes Aquarians tend to lack direction in life, or to get stuck in an unrewarding rut from which even your little bursts of rebelliousness and independence do not extricate you. If that is the case, your dreams will surely provide you with plenty of confinement and frustration episodes, while your occasional escape dream will only serve to remind you of "what might have been." But—what might have been can still be for many an Aquarian. As a matter of fact, sit down right now and compile lists of "assets," "liabilities," "missed opportunities," and "what's next?" We'll wager there will be many entries under assets, one or two big ones under missed opportunities, while the what's next column is so filled you'll need a second page. The point is that you are at your best when you are looking to the future and making plans to implement first-priority aims. Your dreams are probably telling you this very same thing. When we speak of a person finding his or her identity, or determining what the life mission is, this refers to living one's life in a way that fulfills the most positive aspects of that person's individual and unique potential. What is right for a Taurus is not right for you. What is right for a Cancerian is not right for you. As an Aquarian you have your own limitless potential, ever future-oriented, to be realized in your own nonconforming style. Use your own intuition in conjunction with the guidance in this book, and your dreams can get you on your way.

How Do You Dream? Although your life style may demand that you go to bed at eleven and get up at seven, this would probably not be your choice of a sleep period if you had your way. (To bed at five A.M. and up at noon might be more your style!) However, the question of how you dream refers to the content and meaning of your dreams rather than the time slot in which they occur. You Aquarians may not always remember the details of your dreams (until you train your minds to do so), but you are intensely aware of the impression they make on you and of "messages" they may impart. Because it is more natural for you than for some people to see unlikely associations between objects, individuals, or concepts, you will not be long in figuring out that when you dream of late great-uncle Henry, the dream meaning does not concern him at all, but rather your neighbor, whose walk, hat, pipe, or mustache reminds you of the dear departed relative. You will also be quick to spot dream symbolism and relate it to the real-life situation, while your precognitive dreams could have a touch of genuine prophecy. This assumes, however, that you are a positive, fulfilled Aquarian, or at least on your way to becoming one. If you're bogged down by fears and timidity, anxieties and worries, and not utilizing your best talents and assets, you'd probably be as subject to the insecurity-frustration-confinement dream pattern as anyone else. You can learn from these, though.

Confinement Dreams This is the dream in which you suddenly find yourself in a place or situation from which you cannot seem to escape, much as you'd dearly love to. Also, there is no preparatory buildup to your sudden arrival there. Sometimes there is fear associated with this dream, the feeling that something dreadful is going to happen to you unless you get away. In the first place, this is not one of your precognitive dreams and does not mean you are going to experience a real-life situation just like that in the dream. The confinement you feel in the dream reflects either an inhibiting circumstance in your life at the moment (having to work overtime and skip dinner, or having to stay at home with a sick person when you had planned to go out) or a generally restrictive condition in your life (an unrewarding, underpaid job, or a relationship that's going nowhere fast). You feel confined in your waking hours and this is reflected in the dream episode. More importantly, though, the confinement dream represents a restrictive or worrisome situation that you have brought upon yourself, either by sins of commission or omission. A self-imposed confinement, which may be the result of your words or actions in a certain matter—for example, promising a favor that you now find is going to be a real hardship. Or perhaps you broke a promise, purposely or inadvertently, but the end result was a break in an important friendship; again, you were the one who brought the situation upon yourself.

Usually, once you identify the reason for your confinement dream and remedy it, if possible—or take steps to do so eventually—you will not continue to experience this sort of dream.

Insecurity Dreams Once in a while an Aquarian comes along who has a definite predilection for feelings of insecurity. This is rare, but it does happen. These individuals tend to worry about their insecurities in glowing, multicolored panorama, awake or asleep. If you fall into this group, you'll simply have to reorient your entire way of thinking, which is quite a challenge since you'll have to break the habit of years. Most Aquarians, however, experience the insecurity dream no more frequently than anyone else, which is often enough—for this is the most common of dreams. The main feature of the insecurity dream is anxiety; you may be anxious over something that is lost, lacking, or for which you fruitlessly search all through the dream and which you never find. Life being what it is in today's world, people's insecurities often relate to money and other material matters, which is probably why the lost purse, wallet, car, or briefcase is the thrust of this dream. Almost as prevalent is emotional insecurity, which is reflected in this type of dream as the lost child or pet or the person who isn't there when you rush to meet him or her. You Aquarians usually have a healthy attitude toward material security—if anything, you tend toward not being concerned enough about it rather than being preoccupied with the subject. If this is the case, your subconscious might remind you now and then that you *should* be more concerned about material security or that you possibly need to develop a greater sense of financial responsibility—and so, like the rest of us, you'd go through your dream searching for the lost funds!

If you should dream that you are naked or partially clothed when you should be fully dressed, it means that subconsciously you have a gnawing fear of "exposure" regarding some matter. Perhaps you're guilty of some transgression or infringement of the law that you're afraid will catch up with you. In fact, whatever you tend to feeling insecure about in your waking hours is likely to show up in the insecurity dream, veiled in symbolism but identifiable. When you focus on the real reason for your waking-hours insecurity by relating it to the dream, you can then work on doing something about it. But even if you should be unable to erase the cause of your insecurity, the fact that you've brought it out of your subconscious and into the light of consciousness will tend to turn off such dream episodes.

Frustration Dreams This dream is somewhat similar to the insecurity dream insofar as the anxiety is concerned, but the keynote of the frustration dream is the incompleted act. Whatever you're trying to do in your dream is left unfinished when you wake up. Usually it's not your fault (in the dream), as other people or outside forces intervene. You may dream you are trying to tell a person something and he or she disappears before you utter a word—or the dream scene shifts and a nagging frustration sets in because you know there was *something* you should have done and didn't. Or you may be urgently rushing to board a train, plane, or bus and miss it; or you climb stairs all night and never reach the top; or you get to the door for which you've been searching, only to find it locked. Your reaction to frustration in the dream can be your clue to the real-life person or situation that is currently frustrating you, even though you may not consciously realize it. If you are disproportionately upset in your dream over a simple locked door, this may be linked to an opportunity you've been trying to create for yourself in your waking hours, only to have the symbolic door closed in your face. Or the individual in your dream who isn't there when he or she should have been present (after all, you rushed through your dream to get to this person) could represent a friend, relative, or associate who fails you in little ways, and who you subconsciously fear would really let you down in an important need. Again, recognizing the situation or person behind your waking-hours frustration will help you to cope, and also will eliminate the frustration dream from your nightly dream excursions.

Passive Dreams These dreams point up the need for objectivity in a person's life, either as a general attitude or in a specific, current matter. You Aquarians are naturally objective, can be quite detached from emotional considerations, and usually tend to be as impartial about your own life and motives as about other people's. However, once in a while you could get into a waking-hours situation where you lose your perspective because you overreact emotionally and the passive dream will point up the fact. In this sort of dream you observe the action rather than participate in it. You receive the overall picture, without the emotional bias present in the real-life corollary. If you have such a dream, see if it relates to a waking-hours situation in which you have become off-center in your objectivity, as the dream can provide clues to help you better handle the matter.

Action Dreams These are dreams where you are physically active, maybe running, leaping, engaged in a sport, or pursuing a vehicle or individual. Whatever the dream plot, you are—unlike the passive dream—very much a participant. This dream represents either a decisive action you've recently taken in your waking hours or one that you are proposing to take. The key word is action—physical in the dream, but usually involving a decision or innovative move in real life. However, there is also another reason for the action dream, which would particularly apply to some of you Aquarians. We are not saying that you are procrastinators, but occasionally it does take you an awfully long time to make a definite move. You tend to work on the theory that "if I ignore it, maybe it will go away." Waiting for matters to straighten themselves out without your having to get involved can be a wise course, at times, but if you experience an action dream your subconscious is telling you that this may not be the time to wait for problems to resolve themselves. This is when you should take decisive action, make a decision, initiate a new project, or settle a problem. You will find it easier to translate the exhilarating effect of a pleasant action dream into the next day's events. But if the action is unpleasant (if you feel exhausted, discouraged, or physically hurt), then you should consider more carefully a proposed course of waking-hours action, taking into account all possible angles.

Recurring Dreams Recurring dreams may occur frequently or once in a while and may be exactly the same each time or so similar in theme that you recognize them as having occurred before. There is always a meaning—and a message—to the recurring dream, for your subconscious is trying to get a point across to you and apparently you are not grasping it. Symbolism can be a part of the recurring dream. For example, if the recurring dream features the same individual over and over again—and if that individual is not connected with your current life (a childhood friend or a long-gone relative)—then that person is a symbol for someone else who is now involved in your life. His or her appearance, words, or actions, or the environment in which you meet, may provide the clue as to who the individual is. The dream may perhaps concern an object that has a symbolic meaning for you—or it may be the setting of the dream that's significant. You on your way to the marriage altar, for instance, could be significant in terms of your inner feelings about a relationship. Or a party scene could be indicative of a certain group affiliation you have. If you appear as a solitary figure in the dream—alone but not lonely—it could denote your need to develop a creative talent. In any case, there is a valuable message inherent in the recurring dream, so use all your Aquarian intuition to find out what it is.

Escape Dreams This type of dream always represents the subconscious desire to get away from a problem, responsibility, burden, or some especially restrictive condition in your life. The desire is to be free, free, free—which fits right in with your temperament, Aquarius. The content or setting of the escape dream may be varied, but the focal impression of the dream is that you've literally escaped something negative and are into something positive. Sometimes escape dreams feature physical freedom: running away from a pursuer and successfully eluding him or her, hurrying to catch a moving vehicle and then experiencing a wonderful sense of relief and exhilaration when you get on board. A special kind of physical mobility is frequently involved—you can suddenly scale a wall, or jump a great distance, even take right off the ground and fly away. Less frequently, the escape dream is on the mental plane, when you experience a sense of knowing that all is well, or some undefined but vital problem is resolved and you mentally savor the freedom that brings. You'll always recognize the escape dream, whatever its plot, for you'll feel wonderfully free and very happy. The therapeutic value of this kind of dream is evident upon awakening, for you are then in a really great mood to face the day. The positive effects of this dream might even be felt for several days. Aside from your subconscious desire—and need—to escape from a problem or restriction in your waking hours, the pleasant experience of this kind of dream also eases inner tensions. As an Aquarian you might have this type of dream a bit more frequently than most people, inasmuch as you usually tend to crave freedom a bit more than most.

Sex Dreams Basically, sex dreams are simply the result of insufficient, unsatisfactory, or repressed sexual desires in your waking hours, for the more active and rewarding a person's sex life, the less need there is for dream compensation. As with many dreams, there is no logical beginning and the sequence of events is often scrambled or blocked out. Suddenly there you are, in a sexual embrace with someone—very often a total stranger. This could reflect the fact that the sex drive itself is quite indiscriminate. Our training, standards, emotions, and *mental* selectivity determine the choice of sex partners in real life. The subconscious merely gratifies the sexual desire via a dream, with no special focus on a particular person. However, sometimes the individual in your sex dream can represent one to whom you are sexually attracted in your waking hours. In analyzing such a dream you will note certain similarities. You Aquarians can be as unpredictable in your sexual desires, habits, or preferences as you are in other areas of life. You tend not to be "in the mood" when one would ordinarily expect you to be, and very much in the mood at unexpected times and places! This would probably show up in your sex dreams, where your blithe disregard for the conventions is given full play by your subconscious. Your experimental attitude toward life in general could also be evident in your sex dreams.

Sensuous Dreams In this dream your senses are exceptionally keen, and whether you are viewing something, hearing sounds, smelling scents, tasting food, or touching objects, the associated sensations tend to be almost larger than life. If the sensuous dream is enjoyable and makes a deep impression on you, it may have a link with your creative powers. Your subconscious could be pointing up the beauty around you via sense pleasure. It may be that you have an unsuspected talent for art, and when you see vibrant hues in your dream, your awareness of what can be done with color is being accentuated. Or perhaps it's music that's highlighted through sublime or haunting melodies permeating your dreams. You may even be a potential Julia Child, and your subconscious is spotlighting that potential in the food dream! If your sensuous dream is unpleasant, your subconscious is cautioning you against overindulgence of some sort, while the dream that features the sense of touch usually correlates to the need for evaluation. It could relate to a move you're planning to make, or a project you're about to start, maybe a business deal that's in the works. The process of touching, feeling, holding, squeezing, or weighing an object in your hand suggests a need for assessment.

Precognitive Dreams This is the dream that precedes the actual event. Precognitive dreams may be precisely duplicated in a subsequent real-life happening, or they may be realized in essence. In your dream you may be happy and the subsequent real-life event gives you the same feeling of happiness; or you are apprehensive in your dream and a short time later experience the identical feeling of apprehension in your waking hours. You Aquarians are so tuned in to the upper planes, so future-oriented to begin with, that you are very likely candidates for the precognitive dream or for having feelings of precognition during your waking hours. If your waking-hours sense of intuition is highly developed, it is possible you won't have very many precognitive dreams, for whatever is in the forefront of our minds while awake will not tend to show up in dreams. While people do not always realize they have had a precognitive dream until a later event proves it to have indeed been a preview of the future, you Aquarians are inclined to know, even within the dream, when you are experiencing precognition. And unless you are a very disorganized and confused Aquarian, you will not attribute precognitive meaning to just any old dream. You instinctively know when the dream is significant.

Peopled Dreams Everyone dreams of other individuals, but some dreamers see the companions of their dreams in sharper focus than others. There are those who tend to dream of groups of people, none of whom is especially identifiable, while others are extra perceptive to individuals who show up in their dreams. You Aquarians tend to dream both ways! Usually when you dream of a group—or several people—the meaning of your dream will involve a matter of status, social interests or plans, a competitive situation in real life, or a proposed course of action you're about to take. In other words, these people in your dreams are like background material for an event or activity that's essentially oriented around you. On the other hand, dreaming of a specific person invariably concerns a waking-hours relationship, though not necessarily with the person of whom you are dreaming. There will, however, be certain links between the dream individual and the real-life relationship, either through the setting of the dream or the personality or actions of the dream figure. As you know, a person who appears in your dream can also be a projection of yourself. Sometimes when you sympathize with another in a dream, it is subconscious self-pity. Or if you are scolding someone, that person is you, receiving deserved chastisement for something you've done but promptly tucked away in your subconscious. You feel the need to be "punished" but it is a subconscious need, so the dream obliges your instinct for self-preservation by making the other individual the scapegoat!

Symbols in Dreams Symbolism abounds in dreams, but occasionally you will experience a dream episode in which a particular symbol stands out impressively. It may be a single object, an animal, a number, a color, or some sort of mystical pattern or design. You may dream of one of the elements, which are astrologically significant. Fire represents the spirit, earth represents material values, air represents the mind, and water, the emotions. The element of air is especially meaningful for you, as yours is an air sign. A pleasant dream involving breezes, wind, sky-diving, gliding, or other air-related activity would denote a reinforcement of some of your basic ideals and principles. If it is an unpleasant or fearful dream (being buffeted about in the midst of a hurricane, for instance), then the dream means that you are allowing yourself to drift away or be pulled away from those principles that are essential for your well-being. Air- and fire-related dreams are compatible with your temperament and show that (if the dreams are enjoyable) you are balancing spirit and mind to good purpose. If the dreams are negative, then the reverse would be the case. The symbolic meaning of a dream about an animal depends on your attitude toward animals. If you like them, animals in your dream can symbolize friendship or a rewarding experience. If you don't like them, the dream could refer to an antagonistic relationship, perhaps an uneasy truce you've made with an adversary. If you should dream of the number twenty-two (or the number four), the color silver (or a silver object), or any symbol that is analogous to your sign symbol (the Water Bearer) that dream will have special significance, as your subconscious is emphasizing your true identity and, quite possibly, the direction you should take in life.

Chapter 15

Pisces

(February 20–March 20)

Your unconscious state is the realm of your natural instincts and urges, while your subconscious is the area of your deepest desires. Your Sun sign represents the essence of your own, personalized individuality. Because you are a Piscean, your dreams reveal this individuality and the orientation of your own unique unconscious and subconscious states.

PISCES is a water sign, ruled by Neptune, mutable in quality (which means changeable, adaptable). The combination of the water element and the mutability of your sign is reflected in your temperament, for you are impressionable, eager to please, and reluctant to initiate a confrontation. You are versatile in the many ways you find to cope with problems or unpleasantness. Of the four elements into which the twelve signs of the Zodiac are divided (fire, earth, air, and water) the element of water represents subjectively, emotion, and objectively, creativity. Pisces is the sign in which these two factors culminate, for you are the most emotional of all the twelve signs—as well as the zodiacal type most *influenced* by emotional considerations. In the area of creativity, Pisceans lead the field by far, for even if you do not express your creative talents professionally, they are still there, maybe dormant, but decidedly a part of your makeup. Art, music, drama—as well as humanitarian service—are natural "habitats" in which you function at your very best. Neptune, your ruling planet, is reflected in these natural areas of expression for you, and in your romanticism, your tendency to place love above every other consideration, your willingness to sacrifice personal interests in behalf of a loved one. Your deep emotional capacity is in tandem with your sensitivity, which is revealed in your sympathetic understanding of others and, for many Pisceans, in a remarkable psychic ability. This sensitivity also prompts your "escapist" urges, very often manifesting in daydreams and fantasies.

Your Unconscious Instincts You have strong urges to love and to serve. As a matter of fact, there is an ancient astrological precept applying specifically to Pisceans: "Serve or suffer!" That's a bit extreme, but it does have validity to the extent that people of your sign who are engaged in humanitarian service—whether in a full-time career or a leisure-time volunteer effort—derive a personal fulfillment achieved in no other way. The fields of medicine, social service, education, and various forms of counseling have a high percentage of Pisceans in their ranks. This urge to serve also shows up in those who are in the creative or interpretive arts and who give of their time and talent to bring enjoyment or training—to the disadvantaged. The secretary who volunteers a few evenings a week at the neighborhood hospital, or the salesman who spends Saturdays taking kids from the children's shelter to ball games or picnics, each in his or her own way is fulfilling that Piscean urge to serve. Service, of course, denotes a love of mankind; love and service are therefore interchangeable in a sense. In the area of personalized love is found both your greatest strength and your greatest weakness. In a positive way, love can inspire you to accomplish the impossible. Negatively, you can be unrealistic in whom or how you love. The familiar description of Pisces "looking at the world through rose-colored glasses" applies very much to some of your personal relationships, for once you love a person your usually keen perception and intuition tend to be prejudiced by your emotional involvement. While you are indeed capable of being a loyally dedicated lover, spouse, parent, or friend, you can also be taken advantage of by the unscrupulous because of this very quality. Here is where your *conscious* judgments and decisions are important, for although your *un*conscious instincts are to love and to serve, the heavy emotionalism that invariably accompanies love on a one-to-one basis need to be balanced by common sense, certain practical considerations, and the sort of objective thinking which, for a Piscean, must be *consciously* sought.

Basically, nothing could be more commendable than your unconscious instincts to love and to serve, but because the world is not peopled entirely by idealistic Pisceans, these instincts of yours must be recognized, understood, and directed into positive expression by an act of the conscious will. Otherwise, they can be expressed negatively—wasted, misdirected, diverted into channels in which real love or service is bypassed and neither you nor the others involved benefit. These unconscious instincts are constantly at work, asleep or awake, and form a background to your dreams. However, the majority of your dreams are produced by . . .

Your Subconscious Desires Subconsciously, your strongest desire is one that you may frequently articulate: "I just want to be happy!" Of course happiness covers a multitude of areas, but what happiness means to a Piscean is almost always bound up with another individual. Seldom does a Piscean wish for success, money, or power without the even stronger wish for someone to share it with, bestow it upon, leave it to, or work with for its attainment. While there are some signs of the Zodiac that produce people who are self-sufficient, self-reliant, self-involved, Pisces is not one of them! True, if the need arises you *can* make it on your own, you can achieve great success, wealth, and position, but these do not produce the happiness you seek if there is not at least one individual who is close to you. The exception to this is the very spiritually advanced Piscean whose true happiness lies in a life of dedicated service in which personal love is transformed into all-inclusive but objective love of humanity.

In the job or career area, happiness for you is not so much based on the personal satisfaction of work well done (though you can certainly be as conscientious and meticulous in your work as anyone), but on your desire to please another—to make *that* person happy by producing what he or she wanted. Although in your social life, friendships, and group activities yours is frequently the creative force behind various projects, you are happiest when another person helps you to put the plan into operation. It is not that you necessarily need the help, but you do need the supportive presence of another. And you do not mind at all if that individual gets the credit for the project, either.

The fact that your own subconscious wish to be happy is tied in so very often with your dependency on another person—or on his or her dependency on you—is accented by your sign symbol, the Fish. Not just one, mind you—but *two* fish: one facing upstream, one facing downstream, but firmly bound together. While this shows that you are at your best in a partnership situation—a constructive partnership, that is—it also shows your reluctance to break away from another, which is why some Pisceans remain in a totally unrewarding relationship instead of breaking it off once and for all. Sometimes your subconscious desire to be merely "happy" is also tempered with a bit of timidity, a fear of going it alone. Therefore the desire for security (material or emotional) enters into your subconscious. Another secondary subconscious desire of yours is that previously mentioned urge to escape. Even so, these spin-off subconscious desires for security or for escape represent your desire for that special sort of Piscean happiness which, if not found through ordinary channels, is sought in other ways.

In your dreams, whether they are well defined or fuzzy, your subconscious desires are being revealed. Frequently, these will be tied in to a specific desire, though there may be a maze of symbolism or distractions to cut through before the basic desire is identified. Because you have a creative imagination that is given to subtleties and delicate nuances (which is why you Pisceans are such fine artists, actors, and so on), your dreams may often seem somewhat nebulous. However, the reverse may also be true. If your waking life is filled with uncertainty, your dreams may tend to be decisive and clear-cut—the work of your subconscious gratifying your desire to bring a little order to the chaos! Actually, you are probably better qualified than almost anyone else in the Zodiac when it comes to dream interpretation, for you delight in unraveling puzzles, in identifying symbolism, and in spotting the main theme in plots within plots. But you have to be quite objective in this, for self-deception can be your downfall in many ways. In interpreting your own dreams, avoid wishful thinking, and realistically appraise the dream episodes.

Your Special Talents and Abilities These pertain to your conscious state, your everyday waking life.

You may or may not be really aware of your many assets, for you are not by nature likely to have a big ego. This will be particularly true if in childhood you were kept down, discouraged or—most important—were denied the abundance of love, affection, and reassurance so necessary to the Pisces youngster. While such supportive conditions are, of course, necessary for all children, there are those who seem to enter this life loaded with self-confidence and assertiveness. However, Pisceans need to have their self-assurance developed and need very much to know that they are secure in the affections of their parents and family. In case you were deprived of this kind of support, you have had to nurture your own faith in your abilities, and it has probably not been easy. However, you should definitely realize that among your special talents and abilities is the previously mentioned creative force, which can be just as easily expressed through innovative business and commercial ideas as through the arts. You have the ability to maintain idealistic standards even in the face of disillusion, and to stick with a job, project, or a person as long as your efforts are required. Another unique trait of yours is being able to bend but not break under pressure. You have a certain resilience, along with a special sort of patience, which can find you surviving situations in which others would completely fall apart.

Although your talents could very well include those in the entertainment field (dancing is often spotlighted here; Pisces does rule the feet!), there is another side to your nature which shows up in very practical ways. You can be quite security minded and are willing to work to prepare yourself for a well-paying job, with good fringe benefits, by taking additional study courses to improve job-related skills. Sometimes, though, you do tend to stay on in an unrewarding job simply because you can't get up enough nerve to strike out for something better. You are reluctant to burn your bridges behind you—to make the break.

Even when Pisceans are strictly "business" types rather than artistically oriented, they are often very successful in a behind-the-scenes capacity in the entertainment or art fields. The administrative and business end of theater, television, radio, art galleries, photography, and the like are areas in which you are likely to succeed—a point you might keep in mind if you're contemplating a new job/career direction.

Because you are adaptable, versatile, and have a quick grasp of new subjects (this quick grasp is a blend of intuition, osmosis, and your ability to receive impressions that often escape others), you can "fit in" to just about any career, social, or family environment. This is a plus for getting ahead in life, for you do not allow preconceived ideas or stubbornly held convictions to interfere with your making the most of what's at hand. However, it is of the utmost importance that you be realistic in your judgments of situations and people, especially people. Pisceans who part company with reality and follow their impossible dreams, can get carried away by illusory probabilities, messing up their own lives badly, to say nothing of the lives of others. Extreme examples of this sort of thing would be the Pisces woman who leaves her husband and four children to run off with a man who leaves his wife and *six* children, because they claim their love "was bigger than both of us"! Or the Pisces man who trustingly allows a crooked partner to do him out of all his money, simply because he closed his eyes to all the obvious signs of the impending deception (and then proceeds to drink himself to skid row). Admittedly, these are extreme examples—not one in a million Pisceans would do these things—but they do point up your need for objectivity and clear thinking.

As a Piscean, you have tremendous potential for good—not only good in the abstract sense, but the good that comes from the constructive use of your talents and abilities, from bringing happiness to others and thereby gaining it for yourself. Both astrology and dreams are aids in your quest to fulfill your potential. As a matter of fact, it might be a good idea for you to sit down and make a list of what you know to be your talents and abilities. Then make another list showing how, when, and where you've utilized these assets. (Actually, Virgos are the list makers of the Zodiac, but as yours is their opposite sign you can learn from this Virgo trait of concretizing everything in list form, for it shows you right there in black and white just where you stand.) If, by any chance, a bit of indolence creeps into your best-made resolutions, and you devote yourself to eating sweets and watching TV when you really *should* be doing something more constructive, then there's a good chance your nights will be filled with dreams of escape or sensuous pleasure. This is all very well, but as one of your weaknesses is the temptation to move right into the dream world—even when you're *awake*—indulging in the unrealistic could be just too much of a good thing. We suspect, though, that in the midst of your nice little escape dreams, there pops up now and then (just often enough to disturb you) a confinement or frustration dream—your subconscious reminding you that you may be weaving yourself into a cocoon and the time has come to release yourself from *it*!

How Do You Dream? A literal reply to this question might find you stating that you prefer slipping into slumber surrounded by satin sheets, goose-down pillows, and both music and fragrance in the air. But the question really refers to the quality and subject matter of your dreams. In general—because you are basically a creative person—your dreams will be filled with color, symbolism, and sensuous episodes (in which you touch, hear, taste, and so on). However, unless and until you discipline yourself to remember and analyze your dreams, they may indeed be so vague that they blur and slip away from your memory even as you awaken. If you firmly determine as you are falling asleep that you *will* recall your dreams upon waking up, in time you will do so. It might not happen right away, but eventually this does work. Then of course comes the process of figuring out what messages your subconscious is trying to get across to you. Because you are a subtle sort of individual, your subconscious will be equally subtle in projecting its points, and very often it will be the general impression your dream imprints on your conscious mind that will carry the "message"—rather than specific dream events. You may rarely have precognitive dreams. Since you are decidedly precognitive in your waking life, it might be said that there is no need for you to experience this type of dream. Disconnected dream segments may fill your night when your waking schedule is uncertain or disorganized (your subconscious accentuating the disorder, showing you that you should resolve to become better organized).

What Specific Dream Categories Mean to You

Confinement Dreams In confinement dreams you find yourself someplace from which you cannot make an exit. It may be a room without windows or doors—or a cellar, cave, automobile, boat, or any other place that you cannot get out of but desperately wish you could. Although such a dream may include actual physical bonds (ropes, chains, handcuffs), usually it is the *sense* of confinement that dominates, more than specific bondage. This sort of dream has nothing whatever to do with a real-life replica to come. Even if you do dream of being handcuffed, this doesn't mean you are going to be arrested. What it does mean is that you have recently gotten yourself trapped in some sort of situation which you would devoutly like to get out of. It may involve words or actions about which you have a feeling of guilt, or perhaps an unwise commitment you made in an impetuous moment, or long-term payments you agreed to and now find difficult to meet. If this confinement dream stems from any sort of guilt feelings, it may prompt you to make amends, if possible, or otherwise correct the matter. If you have many dreams of this type, it is obvious that there is a condition in your waking life which produces, subconsciously, the feeling of being confined—specifically, a condition which you yourself wittingly or unwittingly brought about. In other words, you are caught in a trap of your own making. As a Piscean you do have a tendency to get yourself into "bondage" from time to time: emotional bondage (restricting yourself and your own development through a somewhat obsessive devotion to another) or material bondage (in which faulty judgment or a weak will impels you to run up bills or mishandle finances). Your own situation may not be as extreme as in these examples, but frequently even a minimum of this sort of thing in your life will produce the confinement dream. As the condition is corrected (or as the monthly payments diminish the bill), you should experience the confinement dream less and less.

Insecurity Dreams These are the most prevalent of all dreams, distributed with equal abundance among all signs of the Zodiac. In this type of dream, you have invariably lost something, or are in a panic because you cannot find or remember something. Or you're about to miss a train, plane, or bus; or you suddenly recall that you've forgotten to do something vital. The dream objects and environments are varied, but your predominant feeling in this sort of dream is anxiety. Sometimes you find yourself without all your clothes on, in a crowded place where—as in the fable of the emperor's suit—no one notices your blushing embarrassment. Most often it is money or a possession that is missing or has been stolen.

The insecurity dream stems from some condition in your waking life about which you feel insecure. Although anxiety about love or money is the most common source of insecurity, in dreams the real basis for anxiety is usually clothed in symbolism. For example, if you have waking-hours anxiety about how you're going to scrape together the cash to meet first-of-the-month payments for insurance, taxes, the car, charge accounts, and a dental bill—all at once—you might dream that you've lost your job. This does not mean you are actually going to lose your job, but merely that the anxiety over financial matters is manifested in your dream as a crisis situation. Or, you might feel somewhat insecure about whether your love partner fully reciprocates your love, and your dream of having lost a prized possession reflects your anxiety that *if* your love partner does not really love you as you do him or her, the relationship might break up (be lost). Again, it does not mean that this is going to happen, but merely that you are insecure in the relationship. If you dream that you are not fully clothed when you should be, it could relate to your feeling of insecurity about some area of your life or about a certain action or condition that you fear may be revealed for all the world to see. It probably never will, but you subconsciously worry about it. However, inasmuch as your Piscean temperament very much orients you toward emotional relationships of one sort or another, your insecurity dreams will usually tend to reflect a waking-hours anxiety of this nature.

Frustration Dreams The frustration dream is somewhat like the insecurity dream, insofar as your own dream feelings of anxiety are concerned, but the keynote of the frustration dream is "interruption." In your dream you never get to finish what you set out to do—whether it concerns transmitting an important message, meeting a person who does not show up, or getting on a train to some specific destination, then suddenly finding yourself in a totally different, alien environment. In brief, your dream intentions are frustrated and you awaken feeling uneasy, cheated, or irritated. Because Pisceans are not the most aggressive people in the Zodiac, you may in your waking hours be especially prone to experiencing frustration. By not competing for a higher-level job, even though you are well qualified for it, you would tend to feel frustrated when a bolder, more assertive, person landed it. Or maybe you are hesitant to develop and utilize a genuinely creative talent you possess, or to assert yourself in a family situation in which you are contributing much more than your share. Such real-life conditions frustrate you, whether or not you are consciously aware of it, and then the frustration theme shows up in your dreams. The antidote to this type of dream episode is to analyze your life style, identify the source of your frustration, and take all possible steps to improve the situation—at which point you will remove the cause for this type of dream.

Passive Dreams In this type of dream you are not an active participant in what's going on, but instead seem to observe it from the sidelines. Rather than taking part in the cocktail party, boat trip, tennis game, or work project of which you dream, you actually view yourself going through your paces. You have the feeling that you're watching a film or TV presentation, and as the action unfolds you're right in there performing, while the real you is sitting back and watching. It is good for a Piscean to experience this sort of dream once in a while, as your subconscious presents you with an overview. In your waking hours, you tend to become personally and emotionally involved with various people and events, and this sort of dream enables you to step aside from such personal involvement and objectively view the total scene. Such dreams will provide clues to whatever conditions in your life require a more detached outlook. If a group situation is featured in your dream, then there is a current situation in your life that requires some degree of emotional detachment so that you can assess the facts realistically. If the dream shows you a picture of yourself in a solitary occupation, then your subconscious is reminding you to consider, objectively, your current aims and plans and how their long-range effect will contribute to your well-being—or the reverse.

Action Dreams You can identify this dream through the very real feeling of motion you experience. In so many dreams, walking, running, or any physical action is softened or diluted into a somewhat fuzzy replica of its real-life counterpart. But in this dream, you actually seem to feel the ground beneath your feet, the stairs that you climb, the air rushing past you as you move along. There is often a sense of urgency in this dream, of fast-paced action directed toward the accomplishment of a specific goal. As a matter of fact, such a dream corresponds to your taking decisive action in a waking-hours situation.

You may have recently made a definitive move (change of residence, job, or relationship), or purchased the ticket for a long-planned trip, or signed up for an educational course. If your action dream is enjoyable, your subconscious is helping you to savor the pleasure of having made a decisive move; if your dream finds you expending much energy but getting nowhere, or if the action is painful or jarring, then you have reservations about a recent course of action you took and your subconscious is highlighting your doubts so that you may further examine the wisdom of your decision.

Recurring Dreams These dreams are always significant, for they represent a fact that must be faced, a condition about which you should concern yourself, or a latent potential you have yet to realize. In the recurring dream, the exact same dream episode may recur now and then over a long period of time. Or the dreams will be strikingly similar in setting, context, and, especially, your own dream reactions. The obvious message in the recurring dream is that there is an important fact or situation that needs attention. Try to recall the details of such dreams, relating them to conditions or relationships in your life. For instance, you may repeatedly dream of something from your childhood—a toy, pet, playmate. If the dream generates feelings of sadness or regret, you may be clinging to an immature attitude toward an earlier stage of your life and this dream is a recurring reminder that you should evolve beyond the limitations of the past. Or you may dream that you are on your way to a specific destination, enjoying the getting there but always awakening before you arrive. When you awaken from such a dream, it is not with a sense of incompletion or interruption, as in the frustration dream, but with a mild curiosity about how the dream would have culminated. At work here is your subconscious pointing up the need for you to pursue a certain goal, which you may desire and have the ability to achieve, but which eludes you because you may lack the impetus to follow-through. Pay attention to your recurring dreams—through them your Piscean subconscious is doing its best to help you.

Escape Dreams This is a category of dream to which Pisceans are particularly prone. Admit it; even in your waking hours you easily slip off into fantasy land, whether you're visualizing yourself spellbinding audiences as prima ballerina in *Les Sylphides* or nestled happily in the arms of your one and only! In your escape dreams, however, the accent is on leaving where you are for someplace different—and better. The overriding feeling in the escape dream is one of freedom, as you exit from a room or building, take off for the wild blue yonder (the dream of flying, under your own power—soaring freely above the earth, unencumbered by gravity—is the escape dream par excellence), or run lithely and *catch* that moving train. The true escape dream is always pleasant, and it almost always means you've a deep desire to escape some real-life burden or responsibility. Your subconscious is granting your wish, and it really doesn't matter what the content of the escape dream is, so long as it produces the wondrous sense of relief from burden, escape from responsibility. Fringe benefits from this type of dream are realized as you awaken relaxed, refreshed, and more optimistic about dealing with whatever it is in your life that you subconsciously wish to escape. Everyone enjoys the escape dream, which comes along all too infrequently! As a Piscean, this dream pampers you delightfully, for escapism is your middle name!

Sex Dreams In general, people who have satisfying

sex lives tend to have fewer sex dreams than those who do not. Any strong drive or desire that is fulfilled in one's conscious state does not really need to be dealt with by one's subconscious. In your sex dreams, the partner who is involved may or may not be the person you are attracted to in real life. True, if you are strongly attracted to an individual, and you submerge, sublimate, repress, or do not acknowledge it consciously, he or she may show up as the partner in your sex dream. However, very often the dream person represents another individual, to whom there is some sort of similarity. For instance, you may be sexually attracted to your married boss, but in your dream it is your brother-in-law, a clergyman, or some other "forbidden" individual with whom you are having sex. The connection would be that the real-life attraction is generally considered morally "out of bounds"—a fact recognized by your subconscious, which substitutes another, equally out-of-bounds sex partner. We're sorry to say that very rarely do people dream of having sex with the partner they actually desire! In one way or another, though, your subconscious does try to gratify your sex drive through dreams—when you need its help.

Sensuous Dreams Over and above the question of sex, Pisceans are among the most sensuous people of the Zodiac. They are "feelers" and "touchers" (rich fabrics, plush furs, velvety flower petals, a baby's skin). Of the five senses—sight, sound, smell, taste, and touch—their sense of touch is most developed, followed closely by sight and sound. This is as true in dreams as in waking life, when the sound of music or the sight of a glowing sunset can send a Piscean up to cloud nine. You *appreciate* sensuous pleasures, tending to savor them as long as possible. Even in eating, you are not the type to bolt down your food, but derive the fullest taste pleasure from each and every morsel. In the sensuous dream the exercise of any of the five senses is much more real than in other dreams, where, for instance, you may have a dream episode of dining with friends, but without really savoring the food. The sensuous dream accentuates each throbbing note of music you hear, each subtle nuance of the colors you see. The scent of the perfume or flower is as real as in life, the feel of the object in your hand as palpable as its waking counterpart. Sensuous dreams, when pleasant, mean that you are aware of, and appreciative of, a recent pleasant event. When unpleasant, such as when in your dream the rose has a thorn that pricks you, or the rich pastry makes you feel ill, or the music is discordant, the dream carries a warning from your subconscious that you are unwisely overindulging in some sense pleasure (not necessarily the one highlighted in the dream). You should be able to interpret this sort of dream pretty easily.

Precognitive Dreams These dreams precede actual events. Frequently the precognitive dream will prefigure the subsequent real-life happening in every detail. Sometimes the events will be important, sometimes not. You may dream that you got a letter from someone from whom you have not heard in years, and the next day the letter arrives (but with no particularly earthshaking news in it). Or you might dream that a co-worker is ill, and shortly thereafter that person comes down with some sort of ailment. Then there are the precognitive dreams which set a mood that anticipates your mood when a later event fulfills the precognition. You may weep in your dream and in a few days be called upon to give comfort to a bereaved friend, or your happiness in a precognitive dream is a prelude to a joyful event in your life or in the life of someone you love.

The precognitive dream cannot always be identified as such until the event that follows reminds you of it—though usually there is a certain feeling in the dream that something significant is being wholly or partially revealed in advance. Because in your waking hours you are tuned in to the higher planes of consciousness, from which stems your psychic ability, Pisceans do not tend to experience precognitive dreams as often as some. When any function, drive, or desire is very much a part of your waking-hours existence, your subconscious has no need to bring it to your attention in dreams.

Peopled Dreams Some individuals dream of crowds or groups of people. Sometimes these people are known, sometimes strangers. As a Piscean, you are not so prone to these crowded dreams. You tend to dream more of a single person at a time, or to dream of yourself alone, engaged in whatever occupation your subconscious dredges up. The people in your dreams can be symbolic (a social gathering might signify your desire to be popular), or the individual about whom you dream may be the "figure" of someone else (dreaming of your parent could represent an authority figure, with the dream actually referring to your boss, teacher, and so on). At times, a person in your dream will represent you. For example, you may dream that a friend is going to make a parachute jump and you are nervous on his or her behalf. This can relate to a daring move you are about to make (a new, challenging job in a different field, or perhaps a residential relocation away from family friends). People in your dream can also represent your awareness of the opinion of others—the "what-will-people-think?" attitude. People in your dreams who are hostile, overtly or covertly, will reflect your concern that something you are doing might not meet with public approval. As with all dreams, you must look beyond the obvious to find the hidden meanings your subconscious is presenting to you.

Symbols in Dreams The people in your dreams, the emotions you experience in your dreams, and the various acts you perform (often completely out of character for you) are often symbolic and actually relate to other matters than is apparent at first glance. There are also dreams in which genuine symbols are glimpsed: an animal, a specific color, a certain number, or an abstract design of some sort. To dream of one of the elements (fire, earth, air, and water) is significant as fire correlates with things of the spirit, earth with material values, air with mental matters, and water with the emotions. The element of water is especially meaningful for you, as Pisces is a water sign. A dream involving an ocean, lake, waterfall, rain, or seeping or rushing water pertains to your current emotional state. If it is a pleasant dream, your emotions would seem to be well directed, healthily under control. If the watery dream is unpleasant, it reflects emotional turmoil, love problems, stress. The element of water also relates to creative expression, which can be an emotional fulfillment for you. To dream of water escaping from somewhere (a leaking pipe, overflowing river, etc.) is your subconscious reminding you that you are allowing your creative potential to be dispersed, to slip away from you. Water-related and earth-related dreams are compatible with your temperament; to dream of both (as in a dream where you are planting flower seeds at the edge of a pool) would meam that you have realized your creative potential and are taking practical, concrete action. Dreaming of an animal will be symbolic in terms of what the animal means to *you.* Pisceans nearly always love animals (particularly strays, who are lucky when spotted by a Piscean and subsequently become pampered pets!), so the animal you dream about can be a symbol of your desire to love. If, by chance, you dislike or fear animals, dreaming of one would be a symbol of uncertainty or suspicion. If you should dream of the number eleven, the color violet, or of a fish (your sign symbol), this dream will have special significance, inasmuch as your subconscious is establishing your inner identity. Such a dream would correlate to your life goals, unique talents, your specific mission in life. Analyze this dream fully for the key to fulfillment.

About the Author

Doris Kaye was born in Cambridge, Massachusetts, and was educated in New York City. She has lived in both Chicago and San Francisco.

The author is a multitalented person who, in addition to having her many articles appear in magazines and newspapers throughout the country, works as an astrological consultant. Ms. Kaye has taken part in several television and radio talk shows, including *The David Susskind Show* and *Good Morning America*.